Understanding China

100 Years of the CPC

Understanding China

100 Years of the CPC

Li Wen

New Classic Press

2024

NEW CLASSIC PRESS

Published by New Classic Press (UK) ★

5th Floor, 99 Mansell Street, London, E1 8AX, UK,

Great Britain ★ Established in the year 2008 ★

Seeking business opportunities worldwide

Understanding China: 100 Years of the CPC

Written by Li Wen

Translated by Amber Navarr, Cheng Si

First published in China by Xuexi Press in 2022.

This translation published by arrangement with Xuexi Press

This English Edition Published in the United Kingdom of Great Britain and Northern Ireland

by New Classic Press in 2024

All rights reserved

ISBN 978-1-915865-81-6

Printed in the United Kingdom of Great Britain and Northern Ireland

B&R Program

10 9 8 7 6 5 4 3 2 1

DESIGNED BY SRA BERKS

The publisher's policy is to use paper manufactured from sustainable forests.

CONTENTS

Chapter I

A Century of Great Achievements

— Why did the CPC issue its third resolution on historical issues on the occasion of its centenary?

When the tides of history surge, pioneers emerge to save the day. At a critical juncture when China was tumbling into the depths of despair and grappling with its future direction, the Communist Party of China (CPC) appeared like a bolt of lightning cutting through the gloomy night sky. Over the past hundred years, the CPC has led the people with the heroic spirit of "daring to make sun and moon shine in new skies", achieving remarkable historical feats and penning the most magnificent and colorful chapter in the annals of Chinese history. As we stand at the juncture of the Party's century-long journey, we cannot help but marvel at its outstanding accomplishments in reshaping the fate of the nation, the people, and the world at large. It is truly a magnificent prospect to see the Party leading the people to embark on a new journey and forge ahead on a new path, as the saying goes, "Its beginning is humble, but its completion will be great."

Delegates to the First National Congress of CPC boarding the Red Boat on Nanhu Lake in Jiaxing (oil painting)

The great cause has endured through the ages, and the glorious era has witnessed a magnificent chapter of a hundred years. In November 2021, the Sixth Plenary Session of the 19th CPC Central Committee was held in Beijing and adopted the Resolution of the Central Committee of the Communist Party of China on the Major Achievements and Historical Experience of the Party over the Past Century (hereinafter referred to as "the Resolution"). The plenary session provides a panoramic review of the CPC's glorious history, great achievements, and valuable experience over the past century. It demonstrates the historic achievements and changes in the Party and the country since the 18th CPC National Congress and calls upon the whole Party and the entire nation to make unremitting efforts to achieve the second Centennial Goal and the rejuvenation of the Chinese nation. This represents a solemn promise of the CPC to remain true to its original aspiration and founding mission, marking a new starting point for learning from history and shaping the future.

1. Needs of the Rejuvenation and Aspirations of the Party and the People

"It is essential to draw valuable insights from the past when examining the current situation, for the present always derives from the past." History serves as a written account and interpretation of human society's past, where historical events have progressed and advanced in a spiral fashion. As such, it is crucial to draw lessons from the history for the present and future. Throughout the vast course of human history, whether it be the Chinese historical masterpieces such as *The Spring and Autumn Annals* (Chūn Qiū), *Records of the Historian* (Shǐ Jì), and *History as a Mirror* (Zī Zhì Tōng Jiàn), or the renowned Western historical texts such as *Homer's Epic*, *History of the Greco-Persian War*, and *Commentaries on the Gallic War*, these records continue to radiate wisdom and provide invaluable insights, despite the historical events being long lost in the depths of time.

The CPC has a longstanding tradition of recognizing the importance of history and drawing lessons from the past in its ongoing practices. In particular, the Party adopted the Resolution on Certain Questions in the History of the Party at the seventh plenary session of its Sixth Central Committee in 1945 and the Resolution on Certain Questions in the History of the Party since the Founding of the People's Republic at the sixth plenary

The ceremony marking the centenary of the Communist Party of China in 2021 was held in Tian'anmen Square, drawing a massive crowd.

session of its 11th Central Committee in 1981. These two resolutions embody a facts-based review of major events in the Party's history, as well as important experience gained and lessons learned. These documents unified the whole Party in thinking and action at key historical junctures and played a vital guiding role in advancing the cause of the Party and the people. Their basic points and conclusions remain valid to this day.

It has been over 70 years since the formulation of the first resolution and more than 40 years since the second resolution was adopted. During this time, the Party and the country have undergone tremendous development, as has the theory and practice of the Party. Today, the CPC finds itself at the crossroads of history and the future, reflecting on the past and looking ahead to the future. It is thus both of objective necessities and with subjective considerations that the Party conducts a comprehensive review of its major accomplishments and historical experience over the past century, particularly since the launch of the reform and opening up.

The Resolution is needed for the cause of the Party and the country. In the century-long journey, the Party has been pursuing its dreams with a passionate heart. The grander the mission, the more magnificent the path; and the greater the challenges, the more glorious the triumphs. Over the past century, the CPC has steadfastly united and led the people in their unwavering efforts, singing a song of national rejuvenation and creating an illustrious chapter in the annals of human development and progress. As we reflect on the past and set our sights on the long journey ahead, we must keep in mind that the surging tide of history is unstoppable and the great path forward is as solid as a grindstone. We must use history to inform our present, and gaze far into the future.

The Resolution is necessary for the unity and solidarity of the Party. Summarizing our history and reaching a consensus on major issues is essential to maintaining the Party's unity. Whether we refer to the first two resolutions, which aimed to "uphold truth and right errors" and to "set things right and look forward in unity", or the present resolution, which aims to "sum up history, grasp the laws, firm up our confidence, and move forward into the future", the purpose remains the same: to unify our understandings, wills, and actions. As we build on the endeavors over the past century to further advance our cause, a deep understanding of the decisive significance of the "Two Affirmations[1]" is necessary to enhance our "Four Consciousnesses[2]" and firmly maintain our "Four-sphere Confidence[3]" and "Two Upholds[4]", ensuring that the entire Party and nation move forward in unison.

A Compendium of Knowledge

"Black Swan" Events

A "black swan" event is a rare occurrence with a low probability of happening that is difficult to predict, yet it can cause a chain reaction and result in significant negative consequences. Such events can emerge unexpectedly in various domains, including nature, economics, and politics, and despite being a chance happening, they can lead to systemic risks and severe outcomes if not handled appropriately.

"Grey Rhino" Events

A "gray rhino" event is a high probability, yet an obvious event that is often overlooked and neglected, leading to a major crisis if not adequately addressed. It can manifest in all sectors of society and is frequently disregarded until it reaches a critical stage, causing a missed opportunity to control or mitigate the risk. The consequences of such events can be severe and far-reaching.

"Jaws" Incidents

A "Jaws" event is a term used to describe an extraordinary occurrence that lies between a "black swan" and a "gray rhino" event. It is a pervasive and devastating incident with a high probability of occurring, and its probability distribution can be speculated, but its exact timing is unknown.

---

1   "Two Affirmations": the affirmation of Xi Jinping's core position on the Party Central Committee and in the Party as a whole, and the affirmation of the guiding role of Xi Jinping Thought on Socialism with Chinese Characteristics for a New Era.
2   "Four Consciousnesses": to maintain one's political commitment, think in terms of the general picture, follow the core leadership of the CPC Central Committee, and act in accordance with its requirements.
3   "Four-sphere Confidence": confidence in the path, theory, system, and culture of socialism with Chinese characteristics.
4   "Two Upholds": to uphold General Secretary Xi Jinping's core position on the CPC Central Committee and in the Party as a whole, and to uphold the Central Committee's authority and its centralized leadership.

The Resolution is essential for the strengthening of our abilities. Adversity makes one stronger, just as polishing makes jade finer. An important reason why the Party remains so vital and vibrant despite having undergone so many trials and tribulations is that we have been improving our ability to resist corruption and overcome difficulties as well as enhancing our aptitude for turning challenges into opportunities by learning from experience. On the road ahead, the further we go, the more complex the environment, the more arduous the tasks, and the more severe the risks and challenges. The emergence of "black swans", "grey rhinoceroses", and "great white sharks" can be sudden and unpredictable. The Party must lead the people in overcoming various visible and potential challenges by drawing wisdom from historical mines, and strengthening our ability to promote social and self-revolution, as well as our capacity to master complex situations and resolve conflicts.

2. Achievements Etched in History, Experiences Illuminating the Future

The Museum of the Communist Party of China stands as a monumental tribute to the Party's century-long endeavors, serving as a spiritual sanctuary that embodies the Party's tradition of revolution in epic proportions. At the forefront of the exhibition hall's display cases, one cannot miss the First Program of the Communist Party of China, written in Russian and with a Chinese translation, which was adopted during the Party's First National Congress. With less than 900 words and even lacking some entries, this document stands as the "birth certificate" of the CPC. A century ago, during a time when various political groups vied for power in China, the founding of the CPC was relatively unremarkable, with few expecting it to achieve the historic greatness that it has accomplished today.

Over the past century, the CPC has led the nation through tenacious struggle, reversing the fate of the Chinese nation in the flood of history. The Party has ushered in a great leap from lagging behind to keeping up with the times to leading the times, creating an extraordinary miracle in the history of the Chinese nation, and painting a magnificent picture in the history of human

The Museum of the Communist Party of China

development. Since the 18th National Congress, the CPC Central Committee with Xi Jinping at its core has led the entire Party and all Chinese people in forging ahead and pioneering innovations, to build a moderately prosperous society in all aspects, and to promote the Party and the country to embark on a new phase. Socialism with Chinese characteristics has demonstrated strong vitality, and the Chinese nation has ushered in a great leap from standing up and growing prosperous to becoming strong. These great achievements made in the endeavors over the past century are enough to be inscribed in the history of the development of the Chinese nation, the history of the development of world socialism, and the history of the development of human society.

A Probe into History

The First Program of the Communist Party of China

The First Program of the Communist Party of China, which was adopted at the Party's First National Congress in 1921, represents the Party's inaugural official document. This document established the name, nature, mission, program, organization, and discipline of the Party. In December 1956, the archives of the former CPC delegation to the Communist International were transferred from the Soviet Union to China. Among the archives was a Russian version of the First Program of the Communist Party of China, which was verified as authentic after extensive examination and comparison. Since then, the First Program of the Communist Party of China has been presented to the world. The picture shows the Russian version and the Chinese translation of the CPC's First Program.

"To understand the great path, one must first study history." The Resolution not only summarizes history and reviews the past, but also pays tribute to history and looks forward to the future. With a comprehensive view of the hundred-year history and a broad perspective spanning the world, the Resolution systematically expounds on the great achievements accomplished by the Party in leading the people throughout various historical periods. By combining historical, theoretical, and practical logics, the Resolution thoroughly reveals the historical significance and experience of the Party's century-long endeavors. It focuses on summarizing the major accomplishments and fresh experiences of the Party and the country in the new era, and clearly puts forward the mission and values of Chinese Communists in the new era. This programmatic document of the CPC, comprising over 30,000 words and divided into seven sections, serves as the "complete collection" and "essence" of all the achievements and experiences of the Party's century-long endeavors.

The Resolution combines a comprehensive overview with a focused analysis. It uses a long historical lens spanning a hundred years to retrace the main tasks and historical processes of the Party leading the people during various historical periods. The document condenses the historical significance and experience of a century-long endeavors and concentrates on reflecting the great path, cause, and achievements created by the Party in the past 100 years. Building on this foundation, the Resolution focuses on the work we are currently undertaking, highlighting the new era of socialism with Chinese characteristics. It devotes a considerable amount of space to summarizing the original thinking, transformative practices, breakthroughs, and landmark achievements since the Party's 18th National Congress, guiding the whole Party and entire nation to strengthen their confidence and embark on a new journey toward building a new era with renewed vigor.

The Resolution summarizes the historical significance and historical experience of the Party's century-long journey. Distilling historical significance and summarizing historical experience are crucial intellectual pursuits that foster learning from history and contribute to the growth of wisdom. With a broad perspective, the Resolution incisively examines the great political, theoretical, practical, and global significance of the Party's century-long endeavors across five dimensions: the Chinese people, the Chinese nation, Marxism, the cause of human progress, and the building of a Marxist political party. Simultaneously, from the perspective of worldview and methodology, the Resolution identifies the decisive factors shaping the development of the Party and the country, and systematically summarizes ten aspects of historical experience, unveiling the underlying reasons and key drivers that propelled the Party leading the people to victory after victory. The complementary nature of historical significance and historical experience enriches the intellectual treasury of the Party and the people, adding to the ideological wealth of a strong Party and a strong nation.

The Resolution explicates the intertwined relationship between the development of practice and the innovation of theory. As great practice gives birth to great theories, and great theories lead to great practice, the 100-year history of the CPC has been a century of upholding the torch of thought while striving to transform the nation's landscape, as well as a century of promoting the integration of the basic principles of Marxism with China's specific conditions and the excellent traditional Chinese culture. Through the integration of the century-long threads of practical development and theoretical innovation, the Resolution makes it clear that the magnificent century-long practice has provided the richest soil for theoretical innovation, and that the ever-advancing theory over the past century has provided the most promising direction for practice. The Resolution is a "practical discourse" that promotes the adaption of Marxism to the Chinese context and serves as the "true scripture" that guides the rejuvenation of the Chinese nation.

The Resolution also highlights the historical logic and practical needs of the Party's past, present, and future journey. "Measure the past events, test them with the future, compare them with the usual, and then decide." All history is the history of the present and the future. Reflecting on history is not to bask in past achievements but rather to better chart the future from the starting point of past gains and losses. Based on the original mission of the Party, the Resolution focuses on the fundamental questions of what the CPC is and what it aims to achieve. It uses the history of the century-long endeavor as a mirror to draw strength from the great victories, learn profound lessons from the setbacks, and achieve the purpose of growing wisdom, enhancing unity, increasing confidence, and strengthening morale. In this sense, the Resolution is a "History as a Mirror" for contemporary China.

3. Grasping the Historical Trends and Seizing the Historical Initiative

From the establishment of the world's earliest political parties, namely the British Whig Party and the Tory Party in the 17th century, the course of party politics over the centuries has witnessed the decline of many erstwhile leading parties and the disappearance of others that enjoyed a brief moment of glory during the tumultuous upheavals of the old world and the construction of a new one. In the end, only those political parties that align with the historical trajectory, comprehend the principles of historical development, and seize the historical initiative can retain their unassailable position amidst the ebbs and flows of change, and remain dynamic amidst a shifting global landscape.

The CPC has endured numerous trials and tribulations, yet it remains a resolute and vigorous force in the face of countless setbacks. The Party's enduring strength is rooted in its ability to navigate the tumultuous historical landscape, gain profound insights into the general trajectory of social development, and steadfastly move forward in the right direction. Mao Zedong's iconic poem, "Qinyuan Chun – Snow", encapsulates the Chinese Communists' astute awareness in discerning the direction of history from the ebbs and flows of power and historical vicissitudes. This poem was composed shortly after the Party Central Committee arrived in northern Shaanxi in early 1936. At that time, the Central Red Army, after hundreds of grueling battles on the Long March, had been reduced in numbers, while the Kuomintang (KMT) was mobilizing heavy forces to mount a siege. In this dire situation, Mao Zedong discerned that the national contradiction between China and Japan had emerged as the primary contradiction in Chinese society, that the CPC was the backbone of the resistance against Japanese aggression, and that they stood on the correct side of history. With conviction, he believed that the revolutionary situation would inevitably undergo a fundamental transformation in their favor, and that the revolution would ultimately triumph.

Reflecting on the century-long journey, it is difficult to identify any obstacle, challenge, or environment that the CPC has not encountered. The Party has surmounted a staggering number of difficulties. During the National Revolution (1924–1927), the KMT reactionaries and warlords brutally slaughtered hundreds of thousands of Communists and revolutionary masses, plunging the revolutionary cause into peril. In the Agrarian Revolutionary War (1927–1937), the disastrous consequences of Wang Ming's "left" deviationist mistakes resulted in heavy losses to the revolutionary bases and forces in the White Areas, almost ruining the revolutionary achievements. The "Cultural Revolution", a decade of internal strife, inflicted the most severe setbacks and losses upon the Party, the country, and the people since the founding of the People's Republic of China, and the lessons learned were exceedingly painful. Nevertheless, the Party persisted in upholding the truth and correcting errors, never faltered at crucial historical junctures or wandered before critical choices. It consistently aligned itself with social progress, seized the opportunity, took the initiative, fearlessly overcame difficulties, and marched towards the light with determination. It can be said that the Party has weathered innumerable trials and tribulations, time and time again, and emerged triumphant from the depths of darkness.

History is the thread that connects the past, present, and future. On the journey towards achieving the rejuvenation of the Chinese nation, the goal has never been as close as it is today, and the prospects have never been brighter. However, the better the situation, the greater the challenges. The more stable the present world appears, the more hidden crises it harbors. The closer we get to our goal, the more tenacity we need to muster. The new Long March is yet to traverse many uncharted snow-capped mountains and vast meadows, and face many unprecedented hardships, risks, and challenges, as well as unprecedented interference, sabotage, and hounding. The future is full of hope, but also full of challenges. Only by maintaining a rock-solid strategic determination, anchoring our goals, and proactively planning our strategies can we gather the powerful energy needed to promote national rejuvenation and create a great work belonging to our generation.

The vast momentum of history is not something we can lead or anticipate but achieving national rejuvenation is an inevitable trend in the development of Chinese civilization for thousands of years. It contains the inevitable logic of world prosperity and progress and represents the trend of the general direction and the people's aspirations. Having gone through a hundred years, the CPC has become more mature in its thinking and more determined in its steps. With unyielding determination to hold onto its goals, the Party will tirelessly drive forward national rejuvenation, remaining vigilant and persistent in its pursuit of progress.

Chapter II

A Grand Epic Witnessed by Time

— Why is it said that the CPC's century-long endeavor has written the grandest epic in the thousands of years of Chinese history?

The mountains and rivers serve as evidence of the passing of time, and in the long history of human society and Chinese civilization, the century-long journey of the CPC is like a fleeting moment. Yet, it has played a profound and historic role in advancing the development of the Chinese nation. A hundred years have passed, and the sea has changed into mulberry fields; a hundred years have passed, and the stars have shifted their positions. The past hundred year has been marked by great change, and the Party has led the people to play a magnificent triumphal ode on the vast land of China, with a powerful melody that resonates through the mountains and rivers. Looking back on the turbulent years of the past, with the rise and fall of dynasties and the vicissitudes of history, the rejuvenation of the Chinese nation is now within reach.

History often becomes clearer with the changes of the world and the erosion of time. Over the 5,000-year history of the Chinese nation, countless dynasties have risen and fallen, and even during the so-called "golden ages" such as the

Cheng-Kang period (1043–996 BC), Wen-Jing period (179–141 BC), and Zhenguan period (627–649 AD) of good governance, as well as the Kaiyuan era (713–741 AD) and Kang-Qian era (1662–1795 AD) of flourishing prosperity, the vast majority of the people remained in miserable conditions and faced many difficulties. Today's China is a land of stunning natural scenery and prosperity, with stability and harmony prevailing throughout the country, presenting a magnificent scene of peace and renewal. We can confidently and proudly say that this prosperous era will shine brightly in China's history and be remembered for thousands of years.

1. Steadfast Commitment to the Party's Original Mission

The fundamental question that must be asked of any political party seeking to establish, invigorate, and strengthen itself is why it was founded and who it was intended to serve, the answer to which reveals its foundation and trajectory. As the earliest form of political parties in human society, bourgeois parties emerged in opposition to feudal autocracy. While they may differ in political tendencies, interest groups, ideological positions, and policy directions, they generally represent the interests of the bourgeoisie and seek to establish a capital-centered political order. In reality, political parties often engage in fierce battles over differing policies and views, such as the "donkey-elephant dispute" in the United States. However, regardless of who ultimately comes to power, it is always capital that wields the most influence and control.

Proletarian parties emerged as the antithesis of bourgeois parties, with their initial political mission being to overthrow the reactionary rule of the bourgeoisie, establish the dictatorship of the proletariat, change the situation of people exploiting people and wealth being possessed by a minority, and realize and safeguard the interests of the vast majority. In colonial and semi-colonial countries invaded by Western powers, proletarian parties are charged with the dual political task of overthrowing the reactionary ruling class in their own countries and achieving the liberation of the people, while fulfilling the historical mission of national independence and national revitalization. As pointed out by the Seventh Congress of the Communist International, in colonial and semi-colonial countries, the primary task of the Communist Party and the working class lies in building a broad anti-imperialist national united front and fighting for the expulsion of imperialism and the struggle for national independence.

The situation in old China was even more complicated as it was a semi-colonial and semi-feudal society burdened by the heavy oppression of "the three big mountains" – the feudal landlord class, imperialist aggression, and bureaucratic capitalism – depriving the Chinese people of their dignity and personality. The labels of "Sick Man of East Asia" and "Chinese and dogs not allowed inside" were extremely contemptuous and hurtful, insulting the once glorious nation and the descendants of Yan and Huang[1] who advocated self-respect and self-love. "Four hundred million people shedding tears together, where on earth can we find our divine land." The people yearned to be liberated and the nation yearned to be rejuvenated, which became the deepest cry of that era.

During the period of the Chinese people and nation's awakening, the CPC emerged like a sounding arrow in the forest and like thunder heralding the arrival of spring, awakening the long-silent Chinese land. The Party fearlessly took on the historical responsibility of seeking happiness for the Chinese people and rejuvenation for the Chinese nation. This original mission has served as the value foundation and practical inspiration for the founding of the CPC. Over the past century, the CPC has remained steadfastly committed to "aspiring to the people's aspiration and happiness", with all its endeavors and achievements aimed at upholding this original aspiration and fulfilling this mission with determination. Throughout the thousands of years of human political development, no political entity has ever made such immense efforts and sacrifices as the CPC in fulfilling its promises to the people and upholding its solemn pledge.

Life is the most precious possession for individuals, yet the Communists are willing to sacrifice everything, including their lives, to fulfill their original

---

1   Yan and Huang are legendary figures in Chinese mythology who are said to have been the ancestors of the Chinese people.

mission. The earliest documented oath of CPC membership contained merely 24 Chinese characters, with the first four emphasizing "sacrificing oneself". The current Party oath places even greater emphasis on being "ready at all times to sacrifice everything for the Party and the people". The word "sacrifice" has been an enduring theme throughout the Party's century-long journey, reflecting the Party's unwavering determination to fulfill its original mission, sparing no effort and even willing to risk everything, including sacrificing their lives. During the revolutionary era, many predecessors sacrificed their lives for the liberation of the nation and its people. Figures such as Chen Yannian, who famously declared "revolutionaries are upright and unyielding, seeing death as returning home, and only standing to die, never kneeling down"; Qu Qiubai, who exclaimed "here is a good place, go ahead and shoot me"; Zhao Yiman, who proclaimed "I do not hesitate to sacrifice my life for the new country, willing to shed my blood to nourish China"; and Liu Hulan, who declared "those who fear death should not become Communists" all demonstrated the Communist Party's unwavering commitment to its mission, even in the face of death. During peacetime, numerous heroes have similarly sacrificed their lives for the prosperity and rejuvenation of their country, giving their all until their dying breath. Figures such as Lei Feng who "put limited life into the infinite service to the people"; Jiao Yulu, who stated "whether in life or death, I belong to Shaqiu Town"; Kong Fansen, who "sowed the plateau with one's hot blood"; and Huang Wenxiu, who "dedicated her life to poverty alleviation", was just one of the countless martyrs and loyal individuals that have had their life and blood melt into the original mission of the CPC, and have vividly

---

A Probe into History

The earliest Oath of Joining the Communist Party of China on record

The earliest recorded Oath of Joining the Communist Party of China was written on a piece of cloth by He Yeduo, a peasant in Yongxin County, Jiangxi Province, during the Agrarian Revolutionary War in 1931. The oath was as follows: "Sacrifice oneself, strictly guard secrets, engage in class struggle, strive for revolution, obey Party discipline, and never betray the Party."

demonstrated the noble pursuit of "greatness in life and glory in death" of the Chinese Communists.

The endeavors of the CPC over the past century have demonstrated its immense value. Without the CPC, the future destiny of the Chinese people would not have undergone fundamental change and the rejuvenation of the Chinese nation would not have been possible. The Chinese nation and its people have chosen the CPC as their leader, and the Party has fulfilled their expectations and earned their trust.

2. Unwavering Faith and Beliefs Even in the Face of Death

Faith explores and resolves the ultimate problems of humanity. Throughout human history, faith has been a constant topic that has played a critical role in shaping the spiritual life. In ancient times, when human productivity, technology, and cognitive levels were low, faith was either sought through religion that "benefits all sentient beings", or through emperors who believed they "inherited the mandate of heaven", or through myths and legends that were "beyond the mundane world" or "mysterious and bizarre". These provided people with spiritual comfort and emotional sustenance in the face of the suffering in the world.

Marx and Engels, who lived in 19th-century Europe, recognized that it was not religion in the Middle Ages that led people away from suffering. Relying on supplication to God provided only temporary relief instead of addressing real problems. They also realized that the development of capitalism has not upheld the dignity and value of human beings. As Marx famously stated, "Capital comes dripping from head to toe, from every pore, with blood and dirt." It generates immense material wealth while simultaneously inducing alienation and psychological trauma in the vast majority of people. Through their profound investigation of the laws of human spiritual activities, Marx and Engels synthesized the world on this shore and the world on the other shore, uniting the real society with the ideal society, the kingdom of necessity with the kingdom of freedom, and developed the doctrine of scientific socialism. The theory contended that mankind could eventually attain the ideal communist society through the socialist movement. This faith in communism has motivated proletarians worldwide to tirelessly fight for liberation and to uphold the noble ideal of justice.

The CPC is not a political group formed out of self-interest, but a union of individuals sharing common ideals and beliefs. The reason why the party is called the Communist Party is that since its establishment, it has inscribed communism on its banner as a grand ideal that it unwaveringly pursues. When British Field Marshal Montgomery was received by Mao Zedong in September 1961, he asked why the Party was named the Communist Party and not the Socialist Party. Mao responded by saying, "Because communism is our highest goal." Thus, communism is the ultimate aspiration of all the Party's endeavors and efforts.

Over the past century, the CPC has faced numerous difficulties and obstacles but has remained steadfast and unwavering. Even if there are thousands of obstacles, we will forge ahead, and even if there is a risk of death, we will have no regrets. Our strength lies in our unshakable belief and unwavering faith in communism and socialism. The Sanwan Military Reorganization[1], which galvanized the military spirit, revolutionized the old army not through high-ranking officials or coercion, but rather through the rallying of individuals around revolutionary ideals and the power of faith to rebuild the army. The towering Mount Baota in Yan'an, the spiritual center of the revolutionary faith, has ignited the hearts and dreams of millions of fervent young people, who would traverse great distances and overcome immense hardships to reach Yan'an City – "Even if bones are broken and flesh peeled off, as long as there is still a breath, we will claw our way to the city of Yan'an." During the Liberation War, millions of KMT troops, influenced by the CPC's revolutionary ideals and political ideas, courageously abandoned their previous allegiance and embraced a new life. During the 1980s and 1990s, when the world socialist movement was experiencing a period of decline, China

---

1   The term refers to the military reorganization program carried out by the CPC in the early 1930s, which aimed to transform the traditional army into a revolutionary force.

remained resolute in its commitment to communist ideals and socialist beliefs. This unwavering dedication enabled China to withstand the impacts of the era and uphold socialism.

The firmness of one's ideals and beliefs depends on whether they can step up and charge forward during critical moments, and whether they can stand firm like a rock in the face of disturbance and maintain their position. Since the 18th National Congress of the CPC, given the unprecedented complexity and challenges in the cause of the Party and the country, and in light of the current state of ideological awareness among Party members and officials, General Secretary Xi Jinping has emphasized the importance of firming up one's ideals and beliefs, referring to them as the "spiritual calcium" of the Communists. He has repeatedly stressed the need to cultivate a "diamond-hard body" and to stand firm as the spiritual backbone of the Communists. This provides the necessary fortitude for the great struggle with many new historical characteristics.

Revolutionary ideals transcend everything else. The century-long pursuit of ideals and beliefs by the CPC is a magnificent journey of spiritual sublimation and a great expedition of spiritual nourishment. Countless Communists have been guided by the beacon of faith. Even though they understand that their ideals may not be realized in their lifetime, they firmly believe that the noblest and most beautiful human belief will ultimately become a reality.

3. Successively Advancing Historical Tasks

"The achievements of our predecessors endure, as we, their successors, follow in their steps." The greatness of history lies in the deep imprint that each generation leaves behind. Each period has its own historical mission and tasks, and each generation has its own historical commitment and responsibility. The development of history is a combination of integrity, continuity, and stages, driven by goals, practice, and values. It is closely linked to the needs of the times, the challenges of reality, and the voice of the people.

The Chinese nation entered modern history amidst the gunfire of Western invaders, enduring multiple internal and external oppressions and experiencing a level of humiliations, calamities, and upheavals that is rare in human history. To save the nation, the country, and the people from peril, various political forces emerged, each with different motives and levels of effort, but ultimately all sought a way out for the nation. In the painstaking search for salvation and survival, Chinese people increasingly realized that achieving national rejuvenation required overthrowing the joint rule of imperialism, feudalism, and bureaucratic capitalism, fighting for national independence and people's liberation, and ultimately achieving national prosperity and the people's happiness.

To break away from the heavy shackles of feudalism for thousands of years and the crushing development gap imposed by Western powers, it was only with the most advanced and resolute revolutionary forces that China could escape oppression and usher in a new era of progress and prosperity. This monumental task fell to the CPC, armed with the principles of Marxism. Over the past century, the CPC has united and led the people to achieve the historical aspiration of national rejuvenation, fight for national independence and people's liberation, and achieve national prosperity and people's happiness. The Party has forged a monumental legacy in the process of the nirvana and rebirth of the Chinese nation.

"To hold fast to one's principles and never give up." The CPC has stayed committed to one theme – the cause of national rejuvenation. The pursuit of achieving national rejuvenation has been the inevitable outcome of China's historical development for over a century and has been the defining theme of all endeavors undertaken by the CPC over the past century. This pursuit is akin to a relay race, wherein each runner passes the baton to the next, and together they progress towards the finish line – the great goal of national rejuvenation. The race is divided into multiple stages, from "creating fundamental social conditions" to "laying the fundamental political conditions and the institutional foundation", from "providing new, dynamic institutional guarantees as well as the material conditions" to "continuing striving toward the great goal of national rejuvenation." With each passing stage, the dream of a rejuvenated China becomes a reality. Today, we are on the great path to national rejuvenation, with a bright future but a challenging road ahead. We must continue to persevere and strive relentlessly, regardless of the obstacles we may face, to ensure that we successfully reach our destination.

"One wave subsides, another rises." The CPC has successively undertaken two major historical tasks – destroying an old world and building a new one, which reveals the general law of social development and progress in Marxist materialistic historical view. It is a necessary requirement for the contradictory movements of productive forces and relations of production, economic base, and superstructure. Following 28 years of bloody struggle, the CPC united and lead the people to defeat various reactionary forces, completely ending the dark history of the old society, achieving national independence and people's liberation, and paving the way for a bright new society. After more than 70 years of unremitting efforts, we have turned a "truly vast expanse of nothing" into an "amazingly prosperous China". A thriving scene has emerged throughout China, where national prosperity and people's happiness are being steadily realized. The two historical tasks, one after the other, are closely related and seamlessly connected, working together to create a better future for the country, the nation, and the people.

"Just as one mountain lets out another mountain blocks, when one challenge is conquered, another arises." The CPC has successively resolved three major social contradictions in different historical periods. Any society is characterized by a multitude of contradictions. As old contradictions are resolved, new ones will emerge, and society progresses by continuously resolving these contradictions. In different historical periods, the CPC has accurately identified the primary contradictions in society and taken them as the starting and focal points for advancing the cause. Whether it is the "conflicts between imperialism and the Chinese nation, and those between feudalism and the people", the "contradiction between the ever-growing material and cultural needs of the people and underdeveloped social production", or the "contradiction between the people's growing need for a better life and the unbalanced and inadequate development", they all reflect China's unique reality and social characteristics under different historical conditions, and highlight the main problems that urgently need to be solved in the times. It is through the successive resolution of these three major contradictions that the Chinese nation has achieved a great leap from standing up, getting rich, to becoming strong.

"The Yangtze River flows on without end." The CPC has strived through four stages of progressive development. Throughout world history, no country or nation has achieved prosperity and strength in one step; rather, such progress is achieved through a positive superposition of accumulated efforts over time. For instance, Germany's rise to power after the Thirty Years' War in Europe took more than two centuries, involving a lengthy process of exploration, unification, and development. The renowned Prussian "Iron Chancellor", Bismarck, once aptly remarked that "the state is a ship on the river of time." Under the guidance of the CPC, the rejuvenation of the Chinese nation has set a course for success, and the ship of progress is sailing forward along the river of time. It has traversed the historical channels of revolution, construction, and reform, sailing towards a new era of broader and grander horizons.

A Compendium of Knowledge

The Thirty Years' War in Europe

The Thirty Years' War, a massive conflagration of European states between 1618 and 1648, was the first all-European war in history, which led to the establishment of European nation-states and marked the beginning of modern European history. This prolonged conflict resulted in the death of 25–40% of the population in the German states, with nearly half of the male population dying. Following the war, European countries formed nation-states, while Germany initiated the process of unification. After prolonged economic, diplomatic, and military endeavors, German unification was eventually achieved in 1871.

4. An Epic Journey with Great Achievements and Challenges

Roughly 5,000 years ago, Emperor Yan and Emperor Huang, considered as the founding ancestors of Chinese civilization, led their people in the Yellow River basin to cultivate the land and start a fire, marking the beginning of the Chinese civilization. On this magical and fertile land, the Chinese people have persevered through countless natural disasters, wars, and conflicts, demonstrating resilience and bravery. With diligence, wisdom, and courage, they have created a brilliant civilization that has endured through the ages, making it a breathtaking pinnacle in the history of human development.

Throughout history, the rise of nations has been fraught with numerous trials and tribulations. When the Chinese nation faced unprecedented changes, the CPC led the people to constantly strive for self-improvement and rise in a struggle. Not only have they prevented the nation from perishing and the civilization from being destroyed, but through long-term arduous efforts, they have allowed the Chinese nation to assume an unprecedented posture in the East, shining with a brilliant radiance in the starry sky of human civilization.

This remarkable journey entailed accomplishing the "two reversals" of the fate of both the Chinese nation and Marxism. The rise and fall of a nation have always been closely intertwined with its ideological foundations, and the fate of an idea has always been inextricably linked to the nation that embraces it. Marxism has reversed the declining fortunes of the Chinese nation in modern times, ushering in a bright future of national rejuvenation. In turn, the Chinese nation has also reversed the fate of Marxism being "terminated", allowing it to gain more penetrating explanatory power and truth. Over the past century, the Chinese nation, the Chinese people, and the most advanced idea, Marxism, have witnessed the convergence of their destinies amid the turbulent changes of the times and the stormy seasons of history. Together, they have played a harmonious and beautiful "symphony of destinies".

This is a remarkable course of action that has led to the "two miracles" of rapid economic development and long-term social stability. The history since the Industrial Revolution shows that economic growth has often been accompanied by colonial aggression, exploitation, crises, stagnation, and social unrest. However, China has chosen a peaceful, independent, and sustainable path of development, relying on its own hard work and determination to improve the lives of its people. It has not followed the path of imperialism or colonial power, nor has it relied on the whims of others or blindly followed them. As a result, China has emerged as a peaceful, civilized, and respected lion in the East that the world is watching with admiration.

This is also a remarkable course of promoting the "two revolutions" of the great social revolution and the great self-revolution. The CPC is a revolutionary party with a strong commitment to transforming both the object and the subject, leading the great social revolution with the great self-revolution, and promoting the great self-revolution with the great social revolution. Over the past century, while promoting social development and progress, the Party has been exploring ways to break free from the cycle of historical rise and fall that is plagued by chaos and turmoil. Through long-term endeavor, especially in recent times since the 18th National Congress, the Party has identified the secret to success: "letting the people supervise the government" through the process of self-revolution. History has proven, and will continue to prove, that only when the "two revolutions" work together and promote each other, can the revolutionary cause thrive and the revolutionary force flourish.

This is a remarkable journey to grasp the "two major trends" of the rejuvenation of China and the advancement of global civilization. Liang Qichao once encapsulated China's development over thousands of years into three phases: China of China, China of Asia, and China of the world. The profound transformations in China's future and destiny over the past century, as well as the historical process of the CPC leading people to seek national rejuvenation, are closely intertwined with the treacherous and tumultuous global landscape. Despite facing repeated invasions, isolation and encirclement by Western countries, subversive hostile forces, or the hegemonism and intimidation of superpowers, the Party has unified and guided the people, not only to survive but also to progress, developing and fortifying itself while also benefiting the world. The achievements and contributions of the CPC manifest not only the responsibility of an advanced political party and vanguard force to the nation but also the responsibility of a century-old party and a major Eastern power to the world.

Young students are reciting poems by Mao Zedong

The journey ahead is as enduring as iron. The past century of glory signifies an exclamation point in China's modern history, yet merely a comma in the grand mission of national rejuvenation. As we traverse the path towards national rejuvenation, facing the direction of the rising sun, gazing at the mountains that stretch like the sea, the scenery is infinite. Though the winds and waves of change may come, we remain undaunted.

Chapter III

A Fierce Struggle with Unyielding Determination

— How was the great victory in the New-Democratic Revolution achieved?

Revolution is the engine of history and a crucial force that propels significant societal transformations. Throughout the thousands of years of human civilization, revolution has been an unstoppable force, propelling the wheels of history forward through the violent struggle of "one class overthrowing another" and through the rise and fall of political power that "accords with the will of heaven and the needs of the people". In modern China, countless revolutionaries stood up and fought to construct a new society and a new nation for the Chinese people. The great revolution surged forward with great momentum, but the road ahead was bumpy. The Revolution of 1911 ended in tragedy and despair with "boundless money, boundless blood, pity those who buy a fake republic". However, under the leadership of the CPC, the New-Democratic Revolution embarked on a new journey of the Chinese Revolution with a new momentum and a renewed spirit.

Over the 28 years of intense struggle for national independence and the liberation of the people, the CPC united and led the Chinese people to find a way through twists and turns, to forge ahead in the face of countless difficulties and perils, and to achieve victories through innumerable trials and tribulations. This has come at an immeasurable cost, with experiences of unimaginable hardships, and the making of unprecedented sacrifices. Today, more than 70 years later, one could only marvel at this magnificent and earthshaking epic, with an upsurge of passion and aspiration.

1. The Revolutionary Force Driving the Current of Change

Workers were striking, farmers were protesting rent, students were marching, and women were offering their support. The progressive forces were gathering and fighting, while the reactionary forces were panicking and trembling. China, a land long oppressed and nearly suffocating, trembled with a fury buried deep in the hearts of the people against imperialism and feudalism. The fury was instantaneously ignited, sweeping across the ravaged land like wildfire and triggering waves of revolutionary fervor that grew stronger and higher with each passing day, forming an overpowering momentum. Awakening from their silence, the Chinese people saw a bright future within reach, with victory in sight.

The Great Revolution between 1924 and 1927 was one of the most socially mobilized and widespread revolutionary movements in modern China. How did the CPC manage to lead and promote a revolutionary movement of such scale and influence just a few years after its founding? What factors contributed to the revolutionary propositions gaining the support and recognition of the vast majority of progressive forces? One crucial point was that the Party set forth a democratic revolutionary program that reflected the common voice of the people and charted the correct course for the Chinese revolution. "Down with the imperialist powers! Down with the warlords!" It was the shared aspiration that united and motivated all the sons and daughters of the Chinese nation.

People in the May 30th Movement

Workers in the Guangzhou-Hong Kong Strike

"Workers and peasants are wakened in their millions to fight as one man." Mao Zedong, Deng Zhongxia, Peng Pai, and other members of the CPC, shed their formal attire and donned more practical uniforms to enter factories, mines, and fields where they integrated with workers and peasants. They promoted and disseminated revolutionary ideas, inspiring the latent revolutionary consciousness among the masses, and resolved to fight against foreign capitalists, feudal warlords, local tyrants, and evil gentry, culminating in a revolutionary thunderstorm throughout China.

During that period, the imperialist powers and warlords had great power and influence, with vast financial resources and weaponry at their disposal, granting them a near-absolute control over the nation. To bring down such a colossal force, it was imperative to unite all possible forces and form the broadest possible united front to achieve the most potent force of justice and to lead the Chinese revolution to victory. Based on this premise, the CPC chose to establish a positive collaboration with the KMT under the leadership of Sun Yat-sen. The joint efforts between the KMT and the CPC resulted in the climax of the great anti-imperialist and anti-feudal struggle, converging into the surging torrent of the Great Revolution.

Amid the revolutionary fervor of the time, few could have foreseen the

---

A Page of History

The Democratic Revolution Program

In July of 1922, the CPC convened its Second National Congress in Shanghai, formulating its primary platform and ultimate goal. The primary platform aimed to end civil strife, overthrow imperialist oppression, achieve national peace and independence, and unify China into a genuinely democratic republic. The ultimate goal was to establish a political system of proletarian and peasant rule, eradicate private ownership, and gradually transition to a communist society. The photo shows the site of the CPC's Second National Congress.

lurking danger and impending turmoil. Under the instigation and support of imperialist powers, the reactionary faction of the KMT and the reactionary warlords revealed their ferocious nature and launched bloody attacks against the Communists and the revolutionary masses. Over 20,000 Party members and nearly 300,000 revolutionary masses were brutally murdered, and the revolutionary cause was cast into a bloody white terror. Mao Zedong bitterly recalled being "slapped to the ground like a basket of eggs, many of us smashed", illustrating the severity of the struggle. Furthermore, as the Party's leading figures made right-leaning opportunist errors, the Party and the people struggled to organize effective resistance, leading to the Great Revolution's tragic defeat.

Mountains become lofty because of their steepness, and great achievements are made through trials and tribulations. Only after the fervor of revolution had subsided did people become aware that the enemy was lurking in the "hidden corners" and had already extended its imperceptible sinister hand to strike a fatal blow to the revolution by surprise. The bloody facts were painful lessons to the young Party. However, countless Communists did not flinch from rising from the ground, wiping the bloodstains off their bodies, burying the

---

A Page of History

The April 12 and July 15 Counter-Revolutionary Coups of 1927

These two counter-revolutionary coups were launched by the reactionary faction of the KMT in 1927. On April 12, 1927, Chiang Kai-shek staged a counterrevolutionary coup in Shanghai, where they wantonly slaughtered workers and Communists. By July 15, over 300 workers had been killed, some 500 arrested, and more than 5,000 gone missing. On July 15 of the same year, the KMT central government in Wuhan led by Wang Jingwei convened a meeting to sever all ties with the CPC and initiated mass arrests and massacres of Communists and revolutionary masses. These events came to be known as the April 12 and July 15 counter-revolutionary coups, which shocked China and reverberated across the globe. The picture shows the arrest of CPC members and revolutionary masses by the reactionary faction of the KMT.

corpses of their comrades, channeling their grief into strength, and regrouping under the Party's banner to wage new battles.

2. A Single Spark Can Start a Prairie Fire

The first shot was fired on the city wall of Nanchang. Then came the Autumn Harvest Uprising, the Qiongya Uprising, the Huang'an-Macheng Uprising, the Battle of Guangzhou, the struggle in western Fujian Province, and the Weihua Uprising, etc. Gunfire echoed intensively, and smoke filled the air. The Communists took up their guns and fought back bravely. The nationwide uprising centered on cities and linked between urban and rural areas quickly pushed to a boiling point. The historical drama of armed revolution against armed counterrevolution continued to unfold. In the difficult journey of the Chinese Revolution, the Party paid a heavy price and eventually came to the realization that "political power grows out of the barrel of a gun", blazing the revolutionary path of seizing state power with military force.

"Attack, attack, and attack again." Retreat is a sign of "wavering". During this period, the erroneous ideas of the Communist International misled some leaders of the Party in believing that launching large-scale armed uprisings to seize big cities would be sufficient to win the revolution in one fell swoop, just as the October Revolution had done. This "left" deviationist putschism fueled the resentment and desire for revenge against the barbaric massacres of the enemy among many Communists, leading to a strong urge to fight for their lives. However, with the combined effect of wrong guiding ideology and irrational emotions, such approach tended to go from one extreme to another. It became clear that with a great disparity in strength, relying solely on passion was of no avail, and unrealistic blind pursuit of radical actions would only lead to a more serious defeat in the end. As a result, the Party was forced to think more calmly about the right path for armed revolution in China.

In the discourse of Marx and Engels, the form of proletarian revolution is violent revolution, relying on the force of the working class, and the path to achieve it is to break out first in big cities, then spread the fruits of revolution,

The August 1 Nanchang
Uprising (oil painting)

The Autumn Harvest
Uprising (oil painting)

and finally overthrow the bourgeois rule and realize the dictatorship of the proletariat. This theory was confirmed by the previous international communist movements. The Paris Commune Revolution that broke out in 1871 briefly established the first political rule of proletarian in human history. In 1917, tens of thousands of workers' Red Guards and revolutionary soldiers poured into the Winter Palace in St. Petersburg, winning the October Revolution and establishing the first socialist state in the world. From the theoretical and practical points of view, the "urban-centered theory" of the proletarian revolution seems to be an indisputable law.

However, in a semi-colonial and semi-feudal society like China, it is impossible to achieve national victory by occupying the central cities. After a thorough review of the experience gained in the Party's revolutionary struggle, Mao Zedong proposed a unique path different from that of the Russian Revolution, based on the China's specific realities. He was aware that since the number of urban workers in China was relatively small, and the peasants made up the vast majority of the population, the control power of the reactionary ruling class in the countryside was relatively weak. Therefore, it was possible to first establish armed workers' and peasants' secession in the countryside, accumulate revolutionary forces, and seize the cities when conditions were ripe, finally winning the national revolutionary victory.

Former site of the Interim Central Government of the Chinese Soviet Republic

Truth is invincible, but the road to find it is bumpy and rugged. The revolutionary theory of "encircling cities from the countryside" deviated from the classical Marxist writings, and there were no existing models to follow. Moreover, the Communist International was not in favor of it. Consequently, some members of the Party questioned "how long can the red flag be flown" and held pessimistic attitudes towards the future of the revolution. Faced with this situation, Mao Zedong, with his remarkable foresight, penned brilliant works such as "Why Is It That Red Political Power Can Exist in China?" "Struggle in the Chingkang[1] Mountains" and "A Single Spark Can Start a Prairie Fire", which underscored the soundness of the path of "encircling cities from the countryside and seizing state power with military force" and predicted the imminent zenith of the Chinese revolution. He passionately described the dawn of the Chinese revolution as follows: "It is like a ship far out at sea whose masthead can already be seen from the shore; it is like the morning sun in the east whose shimmering rays are visible from a high mountain top; it is like a child about to be born moving restlessly in its mother's womb."

Under the guidance of correct revolutionary theory, starting with the Jinggangshan Rural Revolutionary Base opened up by Mao Zedong, revolutionary bases mushroomed in various regions and the Red Army continuously grew in strength. In November 1931, the Interim Central Government of the Chinese Soviet Republic and the Central Revolutionary Military Commission were established in Ruijin, Jiangxi Province. By March 1933, after the victory of the fourth counter-encirclement campaign at the Central Soviet Area, over ten rural revolutionary bases had formed, and four provincial and over sixty county-level Soviet political powers had emerged. Moreover, the Red Army had swelled to over 120,000 soldiers, and the number of Party members had surpassed 130,000.

The relentless advancement of the Party's revolutionary cause had instilled great fear in the ruling clique of the KMT, who urgently marshaled millions of troops to launch an unprecedented attack on the revolutionary strongholds, centered on the fifth encirclement campaign against the Central Soviet Area, attempting to obliterate the Red political power in one swift stroke. Due

---

1   Due to a difference in translation, all references to 井冈山 elsewhere in this book are rendered as Jinggangshan.

A Page of History

The Fifth Counter-Encirclement Campaign

In the latter half of 1933, Chiang Kai-shek deployed a million troops and over 200 aircrafts to launch the fifth encirclement campaign against the revolutionary bases. The campaign adopted the policy of "three parts military, seven parts political". Under the influence of Wang Ming's "left" deviationist dogmatism, the Central Red Army faltered in its fifth counter-encirclement campaign. Consequently, in October 1934, the primary force of the Central Red Army was compelled to abandon the Central Revolutionary Base and undertake a breakout, marking the start of the Long March.

Red Army Climbing Snowy Mountains (oil painting)

Red Army Crossing Grasslands (oil painting)

to the "left" deviationist dogmatic errors committed by the Party's primary leaders during that period, the counter-encirclement campaign suffered a severe defeat. To salvage the revolutionary force, the Party led the Red Army to execute a strategic transfer and commenced the grueling and protracted Long March. This momentous undertaking ultimately augured a brighter prospect for the Chinese revolution, despite the formidable challenges it entailed.

3. The Pillar of Resistance Against Japanese Aggression

Japan has always been a "small and obscure country" to the east of China in ancient times. However, this island nation, which rose after the Meiji Restoration, took advantage of the decline of the Chinese nation and launched a series of aggressive wars that constantly encroached upon Chinese territory.

The September 18th Incident in 1931 saw the Japanese troops occupy Shenyang

The July 7th Incident in 1937 saw the Japanese army occupy Lugou Bridge

The Eighth Route Army and the New Fourth Army, both critical players in the War Against Japanese Aggression, deployed to the front lines in defense of China

The Sino-Japanese War of 1894–1895 saw the occupation of Taiwan, while the Russo-Japanese War caused harm to Northeast China. Japan declared war against Germany, which lead to the forcible occupation of Qingdao and instigated the September 18th Incident and subsequently established the Manchukuo, a puppet government in Manchuria from 1932 until 1945. It stirred up trouble in North China and plotted the July 7th Incident in 1937, which marked the full-scale invasion of China. Through these actions, Japan, greedy like a snake that tries to swallow an elephant, attempted to occupy all of China, and ultimately, achieve its ambition to conquer Asia and dominate the world.

Peng Dehuai in the Hundred-Regiment Campaign

The heroic soldiers of the Eighth Route Army in the Battle of Pingxingguan

The "Secret Base" of the Northeast United Resistance Army

Throughout the Great Wall and across the rivers and mountains of China, the flames of resistance against Japan were ignited everywhere. The Chinese people rose up in an earth-shattering anti-aggression war. The Chinese people united as one to fight against the enemy, rallying together for the survival of their country, for the rejuvenation of their nation, and for the cause of justice for all humanity. They resisted on the frontlines and penetrated deep behind enemy lines, forming an encircling force that entrapped the enemy. The extensive mobilization of society, the profound awakening of the national consciousness, the indomitable spirit, and the unshakable belief in victory all reached an unprecedented height. Fighting against aggression and for the salvation of the nation became the shared will and action of all the Chinese people. In the magnificent nationwide war of resistance, the CPC demonstrated the firmest attitude, the most resolute will, and the most courageous struggle, becoming the mainstay of the nationwide resistance.

The Northeast in distress, north China in distress, and the Chinese nation in distress. As Japanese imperialists intensified their aggression against China, the country was plunged into an unprecedented national crisis. The CPC took the lead in raising the banner of armed resistance against Japan. After the September 18th Incident in 1931, CPC issued the "Declaration of the Communist Party of China on the Japanese Imperialism's Violent Aggression and Occupation of Three Northeastern Provinces", exposing the evil intentions of Japanese imperialism to "turn China into its own colony". In the face of the severe situation of Japanese aggression, which was becoming more and more intense and was causing the gradual loss of our national territory, the Party successively issued the "August 1st Declaration" and the "Ten-Point Program of the Communist Party of China for Resisting Japanese Aggression and Saving the Nation" and launched a widespread anti-Japanese aggression salvation movement, calling on the entire nation to fight against the Japanese invaders. This played a leading spiritual role in strengthening the backbone of the Chinese nation and arousing the fighting spirit of the Chinese people, in stark contrast to the "non-resistance" policy once practiced by the KMT authorities.

Civil war or national salvation? Fight against the Chiang Kai-shek government or alliance with it? Hostility or Cooperation? At the moment of the national crisis, the CPC demonstrated its commitment to national unity and righteousness by prioritizing the overall interest of the nation over ideological differences and past grievances. They advocated for an end to the civil war, unity against foreign aggression, and established and maintained a broad national united front against Japan. They made every effort to promote a peaceful resolution to the Xi'an Incident, to persuade the KMT to change its policy of "internal pacification before external resistance", to push for the resumption of cooperation between the CPC and the KMT, to reorganize the Red Army to join the National Revolutionary Army, and to mobilize the entire nation to defend against the foreign enemy. Under the call of the CPC for a total resistance against Japan, Chinese people at home and abroad worked together and built a steel Great Wall to fight against the Japanese invaders.

Strategic defense, strategic stalemate, and strategic counterattack. In response to the pessimistic argument of "China's inevitable subjugation" and blindly optimistic argument of "China's swift victory", Mao Zedong, based on a comprehensive analysis of the contemporary world and the specific features of China and Japan, proposed a sound judgement that the War Against Japanese Aggression would be a protracted war and that the final victory would belong to the Chinese people. Mao argued that this war would pass through three phases: strategic defense, strategic stalemate, and strategic counterattack, during which the Chinese people's army could leverage guerrilla and mobile warfare in the enemy's rear. Mao's strategic policy of protracted war not only illuminated the proper direction for China's war against Japanese aggression, but also bolstered the people's confidence and determination to ultimately defeat the Japanese aggressors.

The heroes of the Northeast United Resistance Army, the myth-busting victory at Pingxingguan, and the Hundred-Regiment Campaign that elevated national prestige – the military and civilians under the leadership of the CPC were the pillar of the War of Resistance against Japanese Aggression. Martyred generals such as Yang Jingyu, Zhao Shangzhi, Zuo Quan, and Peng Xuefeng,

The commander of the invading Japanese Army presenting the instrument of surrender to the representatives of the Chinese government (oil painting)

along with heroic groups like the "five heroes of Langya Mountain" of the Eighth Route Army, the "Liulaozhuang Company" of the New Fourth Army, and the eight female warriors of the Northeast United Resistance Army, spilled their last drop of blood for the victory of the war. According to incomplete statistics, the Eighth Route Army, New Fourth Army, Northeast United Resistance Army, and other people's resistance forces engaged in over 125,000 battles against the enemy, confronting around 60% of the invading Japanese troops and 95% of the puppet armies in the enemy rear during the strategic stalemate. These forces established a counter-encirclement stance against Japanese occupation of towns and transportation lines, with the backstage battlefield becoming the main battlefield of the Chinese people's War of Resistance against Japanese Aggression. This gradual shift played a decisive role in achieving victory in the national resistance against Japanese aggression.

4. The Song of Victory Resounds Across the Liberated Land

At the outset of the Liberation War in June 1946, there was a huge discrepancy in force between the CPC and the KMT. The KMT had a total strength of about 4.3 million, with a regular army of approximately 2 million, whereas the People's Liberation Army (PLA) comprised only 1.27 million soldiers, including 610,000 field army troops. However, by September 1948, just before the strategic battle of the Liberation War, the KMT's total force had decreased to 3.65 million soldiers, with only 1.74 million being front-line troops, while the PLA had grown to 2.8 million soldiers, with the field army increasing to 1.49 million. What led to such a significant shift in the balance of power between the two sides in such a short period? This may seem to have happened suddenly, but everything can be traced back.

There was a huge difference in leadership performance. War is the highest expression of political power and a concentrated test of political leadership on both sides of the conflict. Through a prolonged period of theoretical and political development, all Party members and the armed forces united as never before in ideological, political, and organizational terms. Any order issued by the CPC Central Committee is executed without fail by the generals and soldiers of the PLA. They obeyed orders strictly and followed Chairman Mao's instruction to "strike wherever pointed". In contrast, the KMT army, despite its apparent advantages in power and number, was factional with each group harboring ulterior motives and pursuing their own interests. They fought a war with subversive intentions, inattentively, and at critical moments were calculating and indecisive. Chiang Kai-shek was "so anxious that jumping up and down would not help". The contrast between "solid steel block" and "loose sand" made the outcome of the war predetermined.

It was clear that the people are for the CPC. On May 1, 1949, Mao Zedong and Liu Yazi had a candid conversation while boating on Kunming Lake in the Summer Palace. During this conversation, Liu Yazi expressed her surprise at the rapid victory of the CPC and inquired about the tactics that were employed. In response, Mao stated that there was no ingenious strategy for warfare; rather, the support of the people was the greatest strategic advantage. The CPC had fought to gain power in order to lead the people out of suffering and into a better life. This sentiment was echoed by a popular folk ditty, which described the people's unwavering support for the CPC – "The last bowl of rice is sent to make military food, the last yard of cloth is sent to make military uniforms, the last old cotton jacket is covered on the stretcher, and the last flesh and blood is sent to the battlefield." In contrast, the KMT represented the interests of a selected group of bureaucratic bourgeoisies and landlords, and was in opposition to the general public. Consequently, the KMT lost the support of the people and public opinion was diminished, ultimately leading to its inevitable collapse.

People sending their sons to join the army and go to the front

Strategic decisions determine success or failure. "Victory is decided a thousand miles away by the strategic planning behind the scenes." The issue of strategic decision-making, traditionally a fundamental factor of military victory and defeat, has been studied by military experts in both ancient and modern times. Clausewitz's "Theory of War", also known as the Western "Bible of Strategy", posits that to win a war with fewer resources, it is necessary to concentrate superior forces in a local formation that exceeds the enemy's forces in both quantity and quality, thus achieving the strategic intent of each attack. During the Liberation War, the PLA focused its superior forces on destroying

The Thousand-Mile Dash into the Dabie Mountains

The courageous PLA soldiers in the Battle of Jinan

the enemy's combat effectiveness, regardless of the gain or loss of a city or location. In 1947, the Red Army led by Liu Bocheng and Deng Xiaoping made a daring move and leaped into the Dabie Mountains, striking at the heart of the enemy, and disrupting the KMT army's deployment. This resulted in the strategic effect of "one move captures the whole game" and secured victory across the entire battlefield. It is considered a "miraculous stroke" in the history of the Chinese Liberation War.

History has shown that justice prevails, and this pivotal moment came swiftly, effectively shattering Chiang Kai-shek's counter-revolutionary regime. The CPC's determined efforts in launching the three major campaigns of Liaoshen, Huaihai, and Pingjin as well as the Crossing-the-Yangtze-River Campaign

---

A Page of History

Three Major Campaigns in the War of Liberation

From September 1948 to January 1949, the PLA waged a strategic battle against the KMT army, which culminated in three decisive engagements: Liaoshen Campaign, Huaihai Campaign, and Pingjin Campaign. The Liaoshen Campaign began in September 1948 and lasted 52 days. It involved the Northeast Field Army and 1.03 million local troops, who successfully liberated Northeast China. The Huaihai Campaign began in November 1948 and spanned 66 days. It saw the East China Field Army, the Central Plains Field Army, and other local forces (totaling over 600,000 men) liberate the East China and Central Plains regions north of the Yangtze River. Lastly, the Pingjin Campaign began in November 1948 and lasted 64 days, resulting in the liberation of northern China. It involved the Northeast Field Army, the Second and Third Corps of the North China Military Region, and local forces of the North China and Northeast Military Regions, who totaled 1 million men. The image below depicts the PLA's victory march following the three major campaigns.

paved the way for a triumphant march to the central south, northwest, and southwest regions, culminating in the decisive defeat of Chiang's dynasty and securing the resounding triumph of the War of Liberation.

Revolution, and only revolution, could liberate China entirely from the humiliations of the past century and successfully usher in a new society. The old system was deeply corrupt, and its destruction required a violent social revolution. The tremendous political force necessary to overthrow the old order stemmed from the immense suffering that it inflicted on the people of old China. In light of this, history and the people of China have chosen the CPC to lead the way forward. The CPC's extraordinary accomplishments in changing the course of history make it a deserving choice of both history and the people.

Chapter IV

Self-Reliance and Self-Improvement

— How was the socialist revolution and construction advanced and achieved?

The crowing of a rooster signifies the break of dawn. The reawakening of the sleeping giant in the East heralds the glorious rebirth of a great nation like a phoenix from the ashes. The ancient and enduring Chinese civilization has opened a new chapter in history, with the long-suffering Chinese people rising once again. The new nation and the new era are not only characterized by a new name and a new starting point, but also by a new landscape and a new spirit. The Chinese nation and its people have risen, not only with straightened backs and hardened wills, but also with a renewed sense of spirit and strength.

That was a time of self-reliance and self-improvement, a time when the Chinese people fearlessly defended their homeland against powerful enemies. It was a time of patriotic fervor and courage, marked by quiet dedication and unheralded sacrifices. And it was a time of unforgettable moments that shook the world and echoed across the globe. There has never been a savior or divine power to rely on; only the generation of self-reliance and self-improvement could build a new socialist China and create a new life for its people.

1. Rising from the Ashes

During the critical period of transition between the old and the new, opposing forces often engage in a fierce battle, resulting in a stalemate. The new forces are determined to push forward historical development, while resolutely destroying obstacles and entrenched forces impeding their progress. However, the old forces refuse to recede from the stage of history and will inevitably make a final, desperate counterattack and last-ditch struggle. After the victory of the New-Democratic Revolution had become a certainty, the CPC faced a complex domestic and international environment. The Party had to unite and lead the people in establishing and consolidating a new people's government, while also completely overthrowing internal and external oppressors and safeguarding the hard-fought gains of victory. This was the CPC's first major challenge as it entered a new phase and sought to solidify its position.

More than 70 years ago, during the founding ceremony of the new nation, the scene was a sea of flowers and a

surge of people. Chairman Mao Zedong stood tall and confident on the rostrum of Tian'anmen Gate Tower, while General Zhu De beamed with joy and Premier Zhou Enlai was relaxed and composed. This unforgettable moment remains as vivid today as it was then. With his powerful Hunan accent, Chairman Mao proclaimed solemnly, "The Central People's Government of the People's Republic of China is founded today." This magnificent statement reverberated through the sky of history, resounding through the clouds, and expressed the victorious joy of the 500 million Chinese people in becoming masters of their own country. Many people were moved to tears when they heard the news, running around to share it with others. Only those who have experienced immense suffering and humiliation could fully comprehend the profound sense of liberation that this day represented. This milestone was the fruit of the heroic sacrifices of China's revolutionary forefathers.

The People's Republic of China had been born, but the newly established people's regime faced a daunting situation, as various challenging problems emerged from all directions. The question of whether they could stand firm and govern the country effectively still lingered in the minds of a significant number of domestic citizens, and some international friends and foes were also watching and assessing the situation. At the time, some capitalists expressed a popular belief that "the CPC had scored 100 points militarily, 80 points politically, and zero points economically".

However, with a relentless and unstoppable force, the CPC was determined to crush anything in its way and eradicate any remaining enemies. When the People's Republic of China was founded, the reactionary faction of the KMT still retained over one million troops stationed in South China, Southwest China, and some coastal islands, while more than two million armed bandits remained hidden in the mountains and forests, presenting a significant challenge. To overcome this challenge, the PLA employed a strategy of large detours, penetrations, and encirclement operations with a thunderous

Following the peaceful liberation of Tibet, the PLA entered Lhasa

force, launching a final siege on the remnants of the KMT military forces. Concurrently, a widespread campaign was launched across the country to suppress counter-revolutionary forces left behind by the KMT reactionaries in the mainland. By October 1950, over 1.28 million regular KMT troops and nearly one million reactionary bandits had been eliminated, and in October 1951, Tibet was peacefully liberated, completing the complete unification of the mainland.

In the aftermath of the war, the primary focus of the CPC was to crack down on sabotage, restore order, and make every effort to stabilize the economy. After the war ended, the areas that were formerly under the control of the KMT government were left in disarray with withering industries and soaring prices. Speculative activities by lawless criminals ran rampant, and the finance and economy were on the brink of collapse. In this context, some people even arrogantly declared that "The PLA can enter Shanghai, but the RMB cannot" and that "controlling the Two Whites and One Black would put Shanghai to death". In order to quickly stabilize the economic order, the Party carefully led a series of major struggles to stabilize prices, unify finance and economics, control inflation and high prices, eliminate the imbalance between revenue

---

A Compendium of Knowledge

Two Whites and One Black

The term "Two Whites and One Black" refers to rice, cotton yarn, coal, and other essential materials that were crucial to the livelihood of the Chinese people in the early years after the founding of the People's Republic of China.

The Huidao Sect

The Huidao Sect denotes a clandestine society of folk believers characterized by unorthodox religious beliefs. While a few of the Huidao Sects disbanded on their own during the early years of the establishment of the People's Republic of China, most continued to operate, and some were even subverted by hostile forces, becoming opponents of the new regime.

and expenditure, and carry out land reform campaigns in the newly liberated areas. The result was a fully restored and improved national economy, with a growth rate of 77.5%, which was 20% higher than the highest level in 1936 before the founding of the People's Republic of China. Even skeptics were convinced that the CPC had great skills in economic governance.

The Shanghai students marched to protest against silver speculation

The Party also focused on cleansing the diseases of the old society, educating the people, and actively advocating new trends. The old and the new societies are like two different worlds. In the old society, people were forced to become "ghosts", but the new society turned "ghosts" into human beings. The Party led the people to implement equal rights for men and women, eliminate "pornography, gambling, drug abuse and trafficking", outlaw the "Huidao Sect", and completely break the old customs left behind by the old society. A mass campaign was launched nationwide to promote the learning of Marxism, and new ideas and new trends were actively advocated, resulting in a new look for society and a marked improvement in the political, ideological, and cultural levels of the people.

In the face of a complex international environment, the Party cleaned up the old mess, started afresh, and took the initiative to open up the situation. At that time, Western countries, led by the United States, held a hostile attitude towards the People's Republic of China and implemented a policy of isolation and blockade. The international environment facing the new regime was exceptionally complex. To deal with this situation, the Party "cleaned up the house before inviting guests" by abolishing a series of unequal treaties and cancelling all imperialist privileges in China. It pursued a proactive policy of "leaning to one side" in foreign affairs, establishing formal diplomatic relations with the Soviet Union and ten other people's democratic countries, as well as with several Asian nationalist countries. All these actions were carried out in an orderly manner, completely discarding the shameful diplomacy of old China and enabling the People's Republic of China to step onto the world stage with renewed confidence and a fresh look.

"Strike hard with a single punch to avoid a barrage of punches later on." The Chinese People's Volunteers (CPV), with great courage and high morale, crossed the Yalu River to resist US aggressors and aid Korea. In close coordination with the North Korean people and army, they launched a series of strategic offensives, including the first battle of Ryosu-dong, the fierce battle of Yunsan City, the battle of Chongchon River, the fierce battle of Chosin Reservoir, and the bloody Sanggamryong Campaign. Through three years of fierce fighting against heavily armed enemies, the CPV emerged victorious, demonstrating China's national and military prowess, and boosting the spirit of the Chinese people. This great victory in the War to Resist US Aggression and Aid Korea, which was a defining moment for China, helped defend the security of the People's Republic of China and showcase its status as a major power. Peng Dehuai, in his "Report on the Work of the Chinese People's Volunteers in the War to Resist US Aggression and Aid Korea", proudly declared, "For hundreds of years, Western aggressors were able to dominate a country simply by setting up a few cannons on a coast in the East. However,

The Chinese People's Volunteer Army resisted US Aggression and aided Korea

that era is gone forever and will never return."

2. Laying Foundation During Transformation

China's path towards socialism was established as the direction and goal of the CPC from its inception, and it was the inevitable outcome of China's historical development. However, in a semi-colonial and semi-feudal country like China then, with its accompanying economic and cultural backwardness, the realization of socialism must be achieved through a two-step process. The first step was to achieve victory in the New Democratic Revolution against imperialism and feudalism. Only then could the country move on to the socialist revolution. The time required for this transition would be determined by the specific circumstances of revolutionary practice.

When the People's Republic of China was founded, the CPC firmly believed that the transition from New Democracy to Socialism was an inevitability. At the time, it was estimated that this process would take "a fairly long time", estimating at least 10 years, and possibly as long as 15 or 20 years. However, unforeseen changes occurred in the socio-economic landscape of China, and by 1952, a significant increase in the socialist component of the national economy was observed, making the transition to socialism more defined and specific. The timing and conditions had become ripe. How did all of this happen, and why?

This was because the Party nationalized bureaucratic capital and transferred it into state ownership, which enabled the socialist state-run economy to flourish and expand rapidly. In the old China under the rule of the KMT, bureaucratic capital controlled the vital sectors of the entire national economy, such as energy, transportation, and banking, while the national bourgeoisie wielded relatively little economic power, mostly concentrated in commerce and light industry, which paled in comparison in terms of proportion, scale, and clout. After the triumph of the New-Democratic Revolution, all confiscated bureaucratic capital was restructured into the state-run economy, consolidating immense economic power in the hands of the state, and endowing this confiscation with the nature of a socialist revolution. By 1952, the output value of state-run industries had soared to 56% of the total industrial output value of the country, and the turnover of state-run wholesale commerce represented 60% of the total wholesale commercial turnover in the nation.

This was because the Party began to regulate the development of private industry and commerce and had already begun the socialist transformation of them to varying degrees. During the New Democratic Revolution, the Party embraced an economic policy that safeguarded the national industrial and commercial sector by leveraging its positive factors while curbing its negative

A Compendium of Knowledge

Mutual Aid Groups, Primary Cooperatives, and Senior Cooperatives

Mutual aid groups were voluntary, mutually beneficial organizations established by Chinese farmers in the early 1950s to address difficulties in agricultural production, such as insufficient labor, animal power, and farming tools. Primary cooperatives are semi-socialist collective economic organizations formed by individual farmers on the basis of mutual aid groups. Senior cooperatives are peasant cooperative economic organizations based on collective ownership of the primary means of production.

ones. As the country underwent a period of national economic recovery, the government implemented several socialist-oriented economic measures to counter disruptions, sabotage, and unlawful activities in the economy. These actions aided private industry and commerce in overcoming production hurdles and strengthened their ties to the state-run economy, resulting in notable changes in their production relations. History often demonstrates that amidst the rush of time, progress may not appear to be actively pursued, but with the momentum of a general trend, it will naturally come to fruition.

This was because we enhanced operational efficiency of the rural economy after the land reform, which promoted the rapid development of mutual aid and cooperation in agriculture in the countryside. Although peasants were allocated farmland following the completion of rural land reform, their productivity was hampered by decentralized labor that made it challenging to cater to the demand for food and industrial raw materials from industrialization, leading to income inequality between the rich and the poor. Therefore, based on the understanding and experience at that time, people believed that organizing mutual aid and cooperation was the way to develop production and ensure common prosperity. During the period of national economic recovery, simple collaborative and mutual aid groups were established, primary cooperatives with land shares started developing, and several advanced cooperatives with collective ownership of the means of production were examined. These changes in rural production relations marked the initial steps towards the development of agriculture in the direction of socialism.

This was also because we faced a challenging and complex international environment, which promoted China to begin to transition to socialism as soon as possible. At that time, Western countries, led by the United States, posed significant threats to China through military aggression, political hostility, and tight economic blockades, making it difficult for the new nation to gain traction on the global stage. During the economic recovery and implementation of the First Five-Year Plan, China only received crucial support from the Soviet Union, which provided much-needed assistance in

Registration of members joining the Agricultural Cooperative

Registration of members joining the Handicraft Cooperative

Celebrating the Public-Private Partnership (the principal form of state capitalism in China adopted during the socialist transformation of capitalist enterprises in the early 1950s)

terms of funds, talent, and technology. In addition, the capitalist countries were facing numerous problems and experiencing a recession, while socialist countries demonstrated much vigor and greater superiority. In this context, we opted to learn from the Soviet Union, the "big brother," and establish socialism as soon as possible.

The Resolution on Certain Questions in the History of the Party since the Founding of the People's Republic of China provides a comprehensive explanation of the historical inevitability of China's transition to socialism from three aspects. Firstly, the socialist industrialization of the country is a natural requirement and a necessary condition for national independence and prosperity. Secondly, the primary contradiction in the country has shifted to the contradiction between the working class and the bourgeoisie, and between the socialist path and the capitalist path. Thirdly, after the land reform, China's agricultural development required the transformation of individual farming into cooperative agriculture.

In a specific time and space, historical synergies converged to drive the People's Republic of China towards socialism. To respond to the historical trend and seize the historical initiative, the Party clearly proposed the general line of "One Industrialization and Three Transformations" and "One Body and Two Wings" during the transitional period. It formulated and implemented the First Five-Year Plan, and carried out the socialist transformation of agriculture, handicrafts, and capitalist industry and commerce in a planned and systematic manner. By 1956, the socialist transformation was basically completed, and most of the primary objectives of the First Five-Year Plan were achieved ahead of schedule. Moreover, with the continuous consolidation of the socialist economic foundation, a series of superstructures such as the socialist political system, cultural system, and social system were also established accordingly. The basic framework of the edifice of the socialist system was initially constructed, and China successfully entered the socialist stage.

Although the development of socialism was a lengthy historical process, it was undoubtedly a monumental achievement. The CPC successfully led the

A Compendium of Knowledge

The First Five-Year Plan

The First Five-Year Plan, which was implemented from 1953 to 1957, marked China's first attempt at establishing a foundation for socialist industrialization. During this period, China launched the construction of more than 10,000 industrial projects and completed a series of key initiatives, ultimately completing socialist transformation. As a result, China's industrial system and national economic system were initially established.

"One Industrialization and Three Transformations" and "One Body and Two Wings"

The term "One Industrialization and Three Transformations" refers to the Party's general line during the transitional period in China, while "One Body and Two Wings" is a metaphor for this general line. "One Industrialization" refers to the gradual realization of the socialist industrialization of the country. "Three Transformations" refers to the gradual realization of the socialist transformation of agriculture, handicrafts, and capitalist industry and commerce by the country. The former serves as the "One Body" while the latter as the "Two Wings".

---

people in eliminating all systems of exploitation, accomplishing the most extensive and profound social transformation in the history of the Chinese nation, and establishing a fundamental institutional foundation for all progresses and development in China. As a result, socialist China had reached a new historical starting point with a new appearance.

3. Building Skyscrapers from the Ground up

China achieved significant breakthroughs in its development of socialism, including the production of the first domestically produced automobile, the opening of the first Yangtze River bridge, the launch of the first large-scale oil field, the birth of the first domestically produced TV set, as well as the successful detonation of the first atomic bomb. China's manufacturing capacity grew from weak to strong, the industrial system from non-existence

1. In 1956, a derrick was erected in the Karamay Urho oil field
2. The first domestically produced *Jiefang*-brand automobile rolled off the production line at the Changchun First Automobile Manufacturing Plant in 1956
3. China's first domestically produced television set was introduced in 1958
4. In 1964, China successfully detonated its first domestically produced atomic bomb

to establishment, the industrial layout from partial to comprehensive, and transportation from scattered to widespread. Breakthroughs were achieved in all areas of society, contributing to the comprehensive development of socialism. The petroleum workers would "rather live 20 years less to take the big oil field", while national defense science and technology workers aimed to "accomplish earthshaking achievement while remaining anonymous". Similarly, the peasants were determined to "rebuild our country and make it prosperous again" with greater ambition. People from all walks of life were full of enthusiasm and vigor, and their determination and hard work were captured in countless heroic moments, many of which were paid for with their lives and blood. These moments became symbols of the spirit of building a new country and a new society. The ten years from 1956 to 1966 were a decade of laying the foundation for China's socialist modernization. These accomplishments not only had an immediate impact on China's economic and social development but also had far-reaching effects that continue to play a vital role today.

Building socialism in an economically and culturally underdeveloped country like China presented an extremely arduous task, given the lack of necessary basic conditions and prior experience. Achieving a decade of success from such a starting point, even with the guidance of predecessors and favorable external conditions, was by no means an easy feat. Moreover, the Party led the people to explore, experiment and constantly correct themselves independently in an exceptionally complex internal and external environment, which is even more commendable. Many things may seem clear in hindsight but were not necessarily so at the time. In the process of exploring and advancing, right and wrong often intertwine with each other, pushing history forward through a complex curve.

To avoid replicating the errors of the Soviet model, the Party proposed a policy of taking the Soviet Union as a reference while independently exploring a socialist development path that was suitable for China's unique conditions. Mao Zedong devoted extensive thought to how to build socialism in China, emphasizing the importance of "combining for the second time[1]" the fundamental principles of Marxism-Leninism with the concrete reality of China, thus creating new theories and producing new works that emerged from our national conditions. Among these, the most notable ones are *On the Ten Major Relationships* and *On the Correct Handling of the Contradictions Among the People*, which signified the Party's new and critical understanding of how to build socialism. As Mao Zedong famously stated, previously, China mainly learned from foreign experience in economic construction, but now we had begun to forge our own path and articulate our own strategy for development.

To eliminate undesirable tendencies in political life and overcome bureaucracy, sectarianism, and subjectivism, the Party launched a comprehensive rectification campaign throughout its ranks. However, as the campaign

---

1   It refers to the combination of Marxism and the reality of China's socialist construction. "Combining for the first time" refers to the combination of Marxism and the reality of China's revolutions.

progressed, a small number of individuals exploited the opportunity to attack the Party and the socialist system, slandering the Party's leadership as "the Party above all" and calling for "power rotation". This abnormal phenomenon aroused the Party's vigilance, and it organized efforts to counter the rightists' attacks. It was essential to take timely action to counter anti-Party and anti-socialist rightists, but due to a misjudgment of the situation, the anti-rightist campaign was seriously exaggerated. This episode serves as a significant lesson in the Party's history.

To expedite the transformation of the country's impoverished and underdeveloped image, the Party mobilized the people to accelerate the pace of development, thereby gaining the upper hand. However, there existed a tendency towards impatience and recklessness in economic development. This manifested in the unrealistic objectives of the "Great Leap Forward" campaign with the slogans "catch up with and surpass Britain in three years and the United States in ten years" and the idea that "the greater the courage of the people, the greater the productivity of the land". Similarly, there was an almost fanatical upsurge of the people's commune movement which mistakenly emphasized the "Communist wind" and pursued communes that were "large in size and collective in nature". Although the subjective intentions were laudable, they contradicted objective reality and facts, producing results that were counterproductive and undesirable. Promptly recognizing the error of this approach, the Party sought to rectify the "left" deviation, and the situation began to improve. However, this process was interrupted by the subsequent "anti-rightist" campaign, which, combined with catastrophic natural disasters and the cessation of Soviet aid, worsened China's already precarious economic situation. To get out of this predicament, the Party decided to adjust its economic strategy, prioritizing the "Four Modernizations[1]" and galvanizing the entire population towards achieving this common goal.

History is shaped by both inevitability and contingency, but ultimately it will move towards inevitability. The process of the ten-year construction may seem complex and intertwined, but the main factors were two threads: the

---

1   Modernization in industry, agriculture, national defense, and science and technology.

correct theories and valuable experiences that the Party acquired while leading the nation in its pursuit of socialism, as well as the erroneous tendencies and profound lessons learned through practical experience. For the ten-year period, correctness and achievement constituted the mainstream of history, while errors and setbacks were the tributary of history. The overall historical development progressed along the first thread. In the subsequent historical processes, although the latter thread dominated for a time, resulting in the Cultural Revolution, the historical momentum ultimately prevailed over the erroneous tendency. Following a major setback, the former thread gained greater momentum, providing the impetus for the creation of a new path for Chinese socialism in the new era.

4. Developing Through Twists and Turns

The ten years of the Cultural Revolution were a period of turmoil, which is a painful memory that remains etched in the minds of the Chinese people and a stern historical lesson that the CPC should deeply reflect upon. Only through a deep understanding of the movement's severe missteps and the harm it caused can we truly appreciate the sense of relief that people felt when it ended. In October 1976, when the "Gang of Four[1]" was overthrown after years of turmoil, the people rejoiced and celebrated with grand rallies and parades throughout the country to denounce the heinous crimes of the counter-revolutionary group and celebrate the great historical victory of ending the Cultural Revolution.

The occurrence of this calamity was not a whim of one or a few individuals, but rather a result of complex and profound social and historical factors. From an international perspective, the People's Republic of China had always been in a precarious international environment. Imperialism had long been hostile and blockaded China, trying to find a way from within to achieve the "peaceful evolution" from socialism back to capitalism. Furthermore, after the rupture of Sino-Soviet relations, the Soviet Union repeatedly exerted great pressure on

---

1   The gang formed by Wang Hongwen, Zhang Chunqiao, Jiang Qing, and Yao Wenyuan during the Cultural Revolution.

China. The danger of external forces subverting the people's government had always existed. From a domestic perspective, the CPC quickly transitioned into socialism after a long and brutal war, lacking the experience in building a socialist society and thus prone to applying the class struggle experience accumulated during the war period to the peace-building period, and to solving problems through large-scale mass movements. Under the influence of internal and external factors, the Party and the country went further and further in the "left" deviationist direction, ultimately leading to this great catastrophe.

In the capital city, people jubilantly celebrated the smashing of the "Gang of Four"

The Cultural Revolution was a period of internal turmoil, initiated by misguided leaders and exploited by two counter-revolutionary groups led by Lin Biao and Jiang Qing, which inflicted severe harm on the Party, the country, and the people of all ethnic groups. During this period, the organization of the Party and state power were greatly weakened, and numerous cadres and people were brutally persecuted. Democracy and the rule of law were arbitrarily trampled upon, and the country was plunged into a significant political and social crisis. This caused the most severe setback and losses for the Party, the country, and the people since the founding of the People's Republic of China, with the lessons learned being particularly painful.

However, we should also acknowledge the distinction between the Cultural Revolution as a political movement and the historical period of the Cultural Revolution. Throughout this period, the Party and the people relentlessly combated "left" deviationist errors, which helped limit the harm caused by social turmoil to some extent. Furthermore, the fundamental nature of the Party, the people's government, the people's army, and the entire society remained constant. Some important progress was still made in building socialism in certain fields. In particular, the accomplishments of the Third-Front Movement were impressive, with numerous transportation routes and oil pipelines constructed consecutively. Additionally, China's defense and civilian technologies made outstanding strides, which played a crucial role in promoting the country's economic development and technological advancement. In the first half of the 1970s, China's diplomatic initiatives charted new horizons, reestablishing its lawful position in the United Nations and marking a second climax in diplomatic relations since the establishment of the People's Republic of China. By the end of 1976, the number of countries that had established diplomatic relations with China had surged to 113, more than double the number at the close of 1969.

In the two years following the end of the Cultural Revolution, the work of

---

A Compendium of Knowledge

The Third-Front Movement

The construction of the Third Front refers to the strategic rear-area construction that took place in the 1960s and 1970s, with a focus on strengthening national defense. This initiative largely remedied the unbalanced industrial layout of old China by relocating a large number of top military enterprises, state-owned enterprises, and research institutes to the central and western regions, which provided rare development opportunities for these regions.

the Party and the state was gradually restored and developed. Errors in certain areas began to be rectified, paving the way for the resumption of normalcy in the country's political and social affairs. However, it was not an easy task to eliminate the impact of the decade-long turmoil in a short period, and the "Two Whatevers"[1] weighed heavily on the Party and the country, impeding their progress. Concurrently, the global economy was experiencing rapid growth, and technological progress was advancing at an unprecedented pace. After a decade of upheaval, the people were eager for the Party and the country to promptly extricate themselves from the predicament and take a significant step forward. In response to the demands of the times and the expectations of the people, Deng Xiaoping personally spearheaded and championed the launch of a profound debate on the issue of truth standards throughout the Party and society. This undertaking had a seismic impact, resembling a thunderbolt rending through the gloomy sky and a spring breeze thawing the winter's ice. It opened up channels of thought and served as a theoretical precursor for the emergence of a new era.

Lenin once used a fitting analogy to describe building socialism as akin to climbing a rough, perilous, and uncharted mountain, where there was nothing that had been tested and proved to be qualified in advance. The challenges and intricacies of forging a path of socialist construction in a vast Eastern nation with unique conditions and a lengthy history were unimaginable. Although we have experienced perplexity, we have endeavored to rectify our course and eliminate deviations. We have encountered setbacks, but these were often surmounted by decisive victories. We have wandered, yet our tenacity has enabled us to break free from constraints and progress beyond limitations, resulting in the continuous sublimation of socialist China amid trials, tribulations, and tests of its new existence.

---

1 "We will resolutely uphold whatever policy decisions Chairman Mao made, and unswervingly follow whatever instructions Chairman Mao gave."

Chapter V

Freeing Minds and Forging Ahead

— How did reform, opening up, and socialist modernization proceed?

"What is socialism? How to build socialism?" These are practical questions of implementing scientific socialism, and questions regarding the mission of a Marxist ruling party. The CPC has continuously sought to answer these questions. In nearly 30 years since the founding of the People's Republic of China, the Party has led the people in laying foundations from the ground up and making explorations amid setbacks and difficulties, thus successfully establishing a socialist society in China and fulfilling the historical responsibility of that time. On entering a new historical period, the Party has continued to lead the charge in freeing minds and seeking truth from facts. Through a combination of positive and negative experiences and amid internal and external pressures, the Party realized that China must follow its own path and build socialism with Chinese characteristics.

By comprehending the logic of historical progress and responding to the evolving trend of the times, we are advancing forward. In the face of global trends, the CPC has successfully steered the country towards the great voyage of reform and opening up. By founding, upholding, safeguarding, and developing socialism with Chinese characteristics, China has caught up with the times in great strides, securing extraordinary historical achievements from the CPC in the new era. Furthermore, the Party has made constant theoretical innovation by establishing Deng Xiaoping Theory, developing the Theory of Three Represents and the Scientific Outlook on Development, and forming the theory of socialism with Chinese characteristics, which provided sound guidance for the reform, opening up, and socialist modernization. All the theories and practices in the new era provide ample evidence that reform and opening up is a crucial move in determining the future and destiny of contemporary China, and that socialism with Chinese characteristics is the correct path toward China's development and prosperity.

1. A Critical Turn and a New Path

When we reflect on the passage of time, certain moments in history stand out for their lasting impact. December 18, 1978, marks a momentous day in the history of the Chinese nation, the Communist Party of China, and the People's Republic of China. On this day, the CPC convened the third plenary session of the 11th Central Committee, marking a great turning point of far-reaching significance in the Party's history since the founding of the People's Republic of China. This pivotal event ushered in a new period of reform, opening up, and socialist modernization.

The great significance of the great turning point lies in breaking free from entrenched stereotypes of thinking and path dependence and opening up a broad road full of vitality and vigor while clearing the fog of thought that had long troubled the nation. The true magnitude of historical events can often only be fully understood when viewed through the lens of the era in which they occurred. Practices that may seem anachronistic today were once ironclad laws, while many modern-day conventions were previously deemed taboo. At a critical historical juncture, Chinese Communists, with Deng Xiaoping as their chief representative, based on an understanding of historical trends and the spirit of the times, successfully created the path of socialism with Chinese characteristics by integrating the principles of socialism and Chinese national

A photo of "all-round contract system"[1] leaders in Xiaogang Village

Yiwu small commodity market in the early stages of reform and opening up

---

1   It was an agricultural reform policy implemented in China in the late 1970s and early 1980s, aimed at increasing agricultural productivity and improving living standards for rural farmers. Under this system, instead of having communal ownership of farmland, individual households were given contracted land and the responsibility to produce a certain amount of grain for the collective.

characteristics.

The path of socialism with Chinese characteristics was premised on the basis of an accurate understanding of the historic juncture. In the past, there was often confusion about the stage of development China was in. There were those who were eager to push towards communism prematurely, while others believed that China was still in a transitional period of intense class struggle. These misunderstandings led to errors of both the "left" deviationist and the "right" deviationist. To avoid these mistakes, the CPC, based on a judicious assessment of the basic conditions of contemporary China, made a scientific judgement regarding China's stage of development. It was recognized that socialism represents the primary stage of communism, and that China is currently in the primary stage of socialism, which is characterized by underdevelopment. This understanding became the foundation for building socialism in China, serving as the starting point for development and the basis for all Party policies and initiatives.

To develop the path of socialism with Chinese characteristics, it is fundamental to firmly uphold the political direction and strengthen the

China's inaugural individual business license

China's first stock certificate

Q&A

Q: What is the primary stage of socialism?

A: The primary stage of socialism refers to the specific stage that China has to undergo in building socialism under the conditions of backward productive forces and an underdeveloped commodity economy. It encompasses the entire historical period from China's entry into socialism to the achievement of socialist modernization. The theory of the primary stage of socialism has two connotations: first, Chinese society is already socialist; second, China's socialist society is still in the primary stage.

Q: What is the essence of socialism?

A: The essence of socialism is to liberate and develop the productive forces, eliminate exploitation and polarization, and ultimately achieve common prosperity.

Q: What is the fundamental task of socialism?

A: The fundamental task of socialism is to develop the productive forces, gradually eliminate poverty, make the country prosperous and strong, and improve the people's living standards.

institutional foundation. Reform should not be seen as straying from the right path by abandoning socialism; rather, it must entail meaningful changes while preserving the core values of the socialist system. Deng Xiaoping famously referred to reform and opening up as a new revolution, which aimed to facilitate self-development and self-improvement of the socialist system while adhering to its fundamental principles. As China continues to reform and open up, it must firmly uphold and consolidate the fundamental system that determines the nature of socialism. For instance, during the process of reform and opening up, it is necessary to uphold the Four Cardinal Principles, namely adherence to the path of socialism, the people's democratic dictatorship, the leadership of the Communist Party of China, and Marxism-Leninism and Mao Zedong Thought. These principles, serving as a guiding light and ballast for the advancement of socialism with Chinese characteristics, must remain unwavering and steadfast at all times.

To create the path of socialism with Chinese characteristics, it is also crucial to challenge existing rules and regulations and introduce bold reforms and innovative approaches. Marxism is not a static dogma, but rather a framework for action that must evolve with changing circumstances and practical experiences. Chinese Communists, with Deng Xiaoping as their chief representative, drew upon their experiences in socialist construction and the demands of the contemporary era to clarify previously ambiguous concepts, introduce novel perspectives, and articulate ideas that were in line with objective reality. Through these efforts, they developed Marxism through a series of fresh and innovative viewpoints on the essence of socialism, its fundamental tasks, development strategies, and development drivers. These novel perspectives included a recognition for development as the top priority, an appreciation for science and technology as the primary productive force, an acknowledgement that a market economy can also be developed under socialism, the use of "Three Favorables" criterions and the Two-pronged Approach, and the policy of "One Country, Two Systems". These vivid and concise assertions are notable for their high degree of penetrative insight, practicality, and explanatory power. They shine with the light of Marxist truth, providing guidance for China's ongoing process of reform and opening up, and becoming the emblematic hallmark and distinguishing feature of socialism with Chinese characteristics.

The opening up of the road to socialism with Chinese characteristics represents a significant milestone for the global socialist movement, marking a new era of distinctive exploration in scientific socialism beyond the confines of a unified model. In the past, there was limited understanding of what socialism is and how to build socialism. However, significant progress has been made in recent times. Under the leadership of the CPC in the new era, the Chinese people have followed the fundamental framework and grand vision outlined by the Party, continuously forging new pathways towards reform, opening up, and socialist modernization.

Q&A

Q: What is the "Three Favorables" criteria?

A: The "Three Favorables" criteria were put forward by Deng Xiaoping during his south tour talks at the beginning of 1992. It includes whether it is favorable to developing the productive forces of socialist society, whether it is favorable to enhancing the overall national strength of socialist countries, and whether it is favorable to improving the living standards of the people.

Q: What is the Two-pronged Approach?

A: The Two-pronged Approach was advocated by Deng Xiaoping, with the two prongs referring to the economic development and promotion of ethical values, respectively.

Q: What is the "One Country, Two Systems" policy?

A: The "One Country, Two Systems" policy means that under the premise of one China, Hong Kong, Macao, and Taiwan maintain their existing system of capitalism for a prolonged period as special administrative regions, while socialism is the prevailing system of the mainland.

2. Upheld Principles and Strengthened the Direction

Over the past century, the struggle between socialism and capitalism has significantly impacted the direction of global social development. The dynamics of this contest have shifted over time, leaving a profound imprint on the world landscape.

In the late 1980s and early 1990s, the collapse of the Soviet Union and the sweeping changes in Eastern Europe sent shockwaves through the world like a domino effect, leaving worldwide socialism and shared human liberation at a low ebb, while the capitalist world cheering up. China, along with a few other socialist countries, found themselves besieged by capitalism and isolated like islands in an ocean, seemingly on the brink of being engulfed and drowned. Some people in China lost faith and became uncertain about how long the banner of socialism with Chinese characteristics could still be raised. Meanwhile, in the West, some voices proclaimed that socialism was a product of the 20th century and would inevitably come to an end in the 20th century. Was it really the end of socialism?

People queuing to buy food after the collapse of the Soviet Union

People demonstrating in the drastic changes in Eastern Europe

A Compendium of Knowledge

Domino

Dominoes are small rectangular blocks made of wood, bone or plastic, arranged in rows at a certain distance. When the first domino is gently knocked over, the rest of the dominoes will cause a chain reaction and fall in turn. A domino chain reaction is the idea that a small amount of initial energy can create a series of chain reactions in an interconnected system.

The End of History

In 1989, American political scientist Francis Fukuyama proposed his opinions in The End of History. He believed that the end of the Cold War marked the end of communism, the development of human political history had reached the end, and there was only one way for the development of history – the market economy and democracy in the West.

Yet, as the saying goes, only in the face of difficulty can one display bravery, and only through determination can one be truly precious. In the face of international and domestic pressures, Chinese Communists, with Jiang Zemin as their chief representative, successfully navigated a series of crises that threatened China's sovereignty and security, consolidated their position, and set the country on the right path towards reform, opening up, and modernization. They overcame numerous challenges in political, economic, and natural spheres, withstood various tests and disruptions, and steered China into the 21st century with confidence and determination.

We withstood the pressure and upheld socialism with Chinese characteristics. China, as the world's largest socialist country, faced intense scrutiny and subversion attempts from the West following the collapse of the Soviet Communist Party. Under the strategy of "pressure for change", western powers waged campaigns against China by political encirclements, economic sanctions, military threats, diplomatic isolation, and public opinion manipulation, etc. They sought to undermine China's leadership under the CPC and dismantle the socialist system in the hopes of replicating the downfall of the Soviet Union and Eastern European countries. Despite the international turmoil, the Party remained resolute in adhering to the basic line of the primary stage of socialism, overcoming a multitude of risks and challenges and stabilizing the overall trajectory of reform and development. The socialist banner remained firmly planted on Chinese soil. China, like bamboo that grows in the cracks of the rocks, stands "firm against winds from every direction, bending but never breaking".

We improved institutions and consolidated socialism with Chinese characteristics. In the face of competition and confrontation with capitalism, it is imperative that we not only fight against capitalism with unwavering determination, but also pursue self-improvement and development through reform to fully leverage the strengths of the socialist system. Failure to carry out necessary reforms will stifle the inherent vitality of socialism and impede its comparative advantages. Under the leadership of the Party, the Chinese people have embraced reform as a powerful driver of economic and social progress, defined building a socialist market economy as an objective of reform and set a basic framework in this regard, and established a basic economic system for the primary stage of socialism under which public ownership is the mainstay and diverse forms of ownership develop together, as well as an income distribution system under which distribution according to work is the mainstay while multiple forms of distribution exist alongside it, further stimulating the dynamism of the socialist system. If we continue to execute these reforms effectively, we can weather the storms of social and economic changes and remain firmly anchored in the principles of socialism. As the old saying goes, "let the wind and waves rise, but remain firmly anchored to the fishing platform."

We opened up new paths and held high the banner of socialism with Chinese characteristics. With progress in reform, opening up and socialist modernization, socialism with Chinese characteristics has been developed with major strategies implemented with great vigor, such as invigorating China through science and education, pursuing sustainable development, and developing a quality workforce. Moreover, we pushed forward strategic economic restructuring, advanced large-scale development of the western region and the strategy of "going global", acceded to the World Trade

The return of Hong Kong in 1997

The return of Macao in 1999

China's accession to the World Trade Organization in 2001

Organization, implemented law-based governance, raised socialist cultural-ethical standards, realized the return of Hong Kong and Macao, and promoted the great new project of Party development, etc. Through a series of strategic deployments and major practices, China has made significant progress in economic, political, cultural, and social development, and the banner of socialism with Chinese characteristics has flown high into the new century. This historic progress can be described as "holding a dream pen to depict a miraculous scene, as the sun breaks through the clouds and the waves turn red for thousands of miles".

Looking back on history, it is evident that the banner of socialism with Chinese characteristics has not only endured, but also been held high, firmly and resolutely. Thus, the history of socialism has not reached its end. And the unflattering views of "the end of history" ended up refuted in the face of indisputable facts and submerged in the surging tide of history.

3. Promoted Development and Enhanced National Strength

In the chronicles of history, each period is marked by symbolic icons that resonate deeply with their respective eras. From the 16th to the 18th National

Shenzhou V manned spacecraft successfully traveling to space

The opening ceremony of the 2008 Beijing Summer Olympics

The opening of the Qinghai-Tibet Railway

Congress of the CPC, the keyword was "scientific development", representing the most contemporary theme. In the new century, China has entered a critical phase of development and reform with highlighted contradictions, presenting a series of new stage-specific characteristics. In confronting these emergent challenges, China has faced new circumstances, contradictions, and problems that it had not encountered before. To resolve these issues and sustain China's favorable economic and social momentum, scientific development has become paramount.

In the face of profound changes in the global situation, national conditions, and the Party's circumstances, Chinese Communists, with Hu Jintao as their chief representative, seized and utilized the important period of strategic opportunity. They focused their energy on development, with emphasis on pursuing comprehensive, balanced, and sustainable development that put the people first. They made all-around efforts to promote economic, political, cultural, and social development, to bolster the Party's governance capacity and maintain its advanced nature. Thus, they created brilliant achievements in scientific development, laying a solid foundation for building a moderately prosperous society in all respects, successfully upholding and developing socialism with Chinese characteristics under new circumstances, and advancing the cause of reform, opening up, and socialist modernization to a new stage of development.

China's economic capability reached a new level. From 2002 to 2012, China's social productivity, economic strength, and scientific and technological prowess surged rapidly. Its GDP increased from more than 12 trillion yuan to over 50 trillion yuan, with per capita GDP rising from over 1,000 USD to more than 6,000 USD. China's economic size jumped from sixth to second place globally, occupying a pivotal position in the world economic pattern. China made remarkable scientific and technological achievements, such as the manned space program, the lunar exploration program, and supercomputing, and succeeded in a series of major engineering feats, such as the Qinghai-Tibet Railway, Three Gorges Dam, and South-to-North Water Diversion Project. China also successfully overcame major challenges, including the SARS epidemic and the great earthquake disaster, and hosted major events such as the Beijing Summer Olympics and Paralympics. These accomplishments have transformed China's landscape rapidly.

Chinese people's living standards ascended to a new level. With the country's economic strength on the rise, the living standards of hundreds of millions of people have improved rapidly, and efforts to safeguard and enhance the well-being of the people have intensified, resulting in a historic leap from subsistence to moderate prosperity in general. The practice of "national grain tax", which had persisted for thousands of years, has now become a thing of the past. Furthermore, all tuition and incidental fees for compulsory education have been exempted, and the social security safety net has been fortified. By 2012, the number of individuals covered by various pension insurance schemes had reached 790 million, while the number of people insured under

1.Low-income households exhibiting their subsistence allowance certificates
2.A contented pupil after the exemption of tuition and incidental fees
3.A jubilant farmer following the exemption of agricultural taxes
4.Elderly rural residents receiving their pensions

The South-North Water Diversion Project

The Three Gorges Dam Project

The West-East Gas Transmission Project

different medical insurance plans exceeded 1.3 billion. Essentially, China has basically established the world's largest social security system in terms of population coverage.

China's international influence scaled new heights. As China has developed, its influence on the world stage has grown significantly, making increasing contributions to global peace and development. China has pursued a foreign policy that emphasizes extensive bilateral and multilateral diplomacy, forging friendly and cooperative relations with countries around the world. Through its active participation in international affairs, China has played a constructive role in mediating international disputes and conflicts, and in responding to the global financial crisis and the European debt crisis. Moreover, China has aided third-world countries in areas such as counter-terrorism, environmental protection, anti-drug efforts, and the prevention and treatment of major diseases, building its image as a responsible major country.

"Seemingly ordinary, yet the most remarkable, achieving it seems easy but is actually difficult." The rapid development of the cause of the Party and the country during this period is the result of overcoming a series of major challenges. China has handled unexpected emergencies and difficulties, overcome unprecedented disasters and catastrophes, and accomplished a series of major events and projects, which consolidated and developed the overall situation of reform, opening up, and socialist modernization. The extraordinary journey and vivid practice have demonstrated the unparalleled strengths of socialism with Chinese characteristics and enhanced the pride and cohesion of the Chinese people and the Chinese nation.

It hasn't been long, and the memories remain fresh. Reflecting on the history of the past three decades in the new era, we sincerely recognize the significant impact of the unprecedented great reform and opening up. It has enabled the Chinese nation to make great strides towards its rejuvenation, empowered socialism with Chinese characteristics to demonstrate its vitality and strong leadership, and enabled world socialism, after encountering setbacks, to rekindle its vigor.

Chapter VI

Upholding Fundamental Principles and Breaking New Ground

— How was the new era of socialism with Chinese characteristics opened?

On the river of time, each era supersedes the previous one, and history keeps marching forward like waves beating against the shore. In the long-term development of Chinese society, there has always been a phenomenon known as "leapfrog mutation". The new era of socialism with Chinese characteristics marks a new height in the historical process of the rejuvenation of the Chinese nation, with its new historical position, mission and spirit. It has created a new epoch of progress in human civilization.

The rising of the Chinese nation resembles the ascending of the eternal sun and moon. Standing at this great historical juncture, Chinese Communists, with Xi Jinping as their chief representative, have demonstrated great courage, wisdom, and strength in uniting the people and leading them to sing the magnificent triumphal song of "the red flag flutters over the grand passes" and write a glorious chapter of "hoisting the sails to cross the sea". In this new era of vigorous and determined endeavor, we are not merely witnesses but also active participants, feeling the pulse of the times, sensing the rhythm of history, and contributing to the glory of the era, thus creating a brilliant history.

1. Scientific Support for the Judgement of a New Era

The era, due to its unique characteristics, such as practical background, primary contradictions, production conditions, and spiritual outlook, is not only an objective concept of time but also holds significant socio-historical meaning. Throughout the long evolution of human society from backwardness to progress and from ignorance to civilization, distinct historical imprints and

Beijing Daxing International Airport

China High-Speed Rail

Shanghai Pilot Free Trade Zone

Silk Road Golden Bridge

epochal marks have been left behind in different eras, whether it is the Stone Age, the Agrarian Age, the Steam Age, the Electric Age, and the Information Age, marked by revolutions in modes of production, or the Pre-Globalization Age, the Great Naval Age, the Great Colonial Age, the Great Emancipation Age, and the Age of Great Change, which were characterized by changes in production activities. These eras have become significant milestones in the process of world civilization.

Looking at it from this broader perspective, one can gain a more comprehensive and profound understanding of the historical inevitability and scientific rationality of China's entry into a new era of socialism with Chinese characteristics. This major judgment represents a scientific conclusion drawn

The new look of agriculture, rural areas and farmers in the New Era

from the historical trends observed from the continuity of Chinese civilization for over 5,000 years, the efforts to achieve national rejuvenation over more than a century, the interaction between China and the world for the past 180 years of modern times, as well as the power struggle between socialism and capitalism over the last century.

Scientific judgment stems from seizing the initiative of history. China is an ancient nation with a long-standing and splendid civilization. However, in the modern era, the Chinese nation and civilization experienced a gradual recession, necessitating a historical process of "momentum accumulation" to reverse this destiny. The long march towards achieving a grand goal often requires a few critical steps. After more than a century of tireless efforts by the Chinese people, the "rebound curve" for national rejuvenation and cultural revitalization has reached a critical stage of momentum gathering. The new era is a great era that marks the accomplishment of the First Centenary Goal and embarks on a new journey towards achieving the Second Centenary Goal, elevating the great cause of national rejuvenation to a higher level.

Scientific judgment arises from adapting to the needs of reality. Since the advent of modern times, many countries have faced the challenge of making a "risky leap" in development. Some have successfully navigated this transition to ascend to higher stages of development, while others have struggled and fallen into long-term stagnation or even regression. After experiencing a prolonged period of rapid development through reform and opening up, China's economy has been soaring, with an economic growth rate of 10.6% and its economic aggregate rising to a second place in the world by 2010. However, the drawbacks of the traditional development model, characterized by extensive growth, have become increasingly apparent. Constraints related to population, resources, and the environment are tightening, and the dividends that had supported development are declining, making it clear that the driving force for development is insufficient. The new era is one of transformation, where development modes must be shifted, advantages strengthened, and momentum enhanced to achieve high-speed growth and high-quality development, thus elevating economic and social development to new heights.

Scientific judgment derives from discerning the transformation of contradictions. The movement of contradictions is the driving force behind social progress, and the fundamental contradiction plays a decisive role. Resolving the old major contradiction plays a pivotal role in liberating society from its previous fetters, while the new major contradiction becomes the focus of efforts to push for progress. China's socialist project was initiated in the context of an extremely backward economy and culture, and for a long time, the principal contradiction in society lay between the growing material and cultural needs of the people and the underdeveloped social production system. Today, both sides of the main social contradiction have changed, and the disparity between the people's ever-growing needs for a better life and the unbalanced and inadequate development has become increasingly conspicuous. Addressing this contradiction has become our primary objective for the present and the future. The new era is a momentous epoch that aims to meet people's expectations for a higher quality of life, to enhance the comprehensiveness and balance of development, and to elevate the driving force for social progress to a higher stage.

Scientific judgment comes from having insight into the global trends. China is now closer than ever to the center of the world stage, attracting significant attention from around the world. The relationship between China and the world has undergone profound changes. In the context of the world's great development, transformation, and adjustment, Chinese ideas, propositions, and wisdom are emerging as vital solutions to global challenges. China's strength, responsibility, and contributions are becoming the key variables influencing the development of the world. The new era is a significant period to open up a new paradigm for China's diplomacy as a major country, to continuously expand its national influence and leadership, and to elevate China's international status to a higher level.

2. Rich Connotations of the New Era

The Chinese nation once had an extraordinary grandeur of "opening the palace in the heavens and accepting the worship of all nations". However, during the modern era, our imagination was limited by our weakness. Even the bold visions put forth by Liang Qichao's *The Future of New China* (Xīn Zhōng Guó Wèi Lái Jì), Jin Zuotong's *The New Era* (Xīn Jì Yuán), and Lu Shi'e's *The New China* (Xīn Zhōng Guó) in the late Qing Dynasty and early Republican period were only imaginations of how China could survive and develop within the constraints of the old world system. Today, people living in this great new era feel an infinite sense of regret for our ancestors who lacked the grand vision and broad-mindedness to navigate the troubled times of their day. Yet we now have the freedom to imagine the vast horizons and bright prospects of China's future development.

The new era is a great time for the Chinese nation to display its grand plans, for the CPC to forge ahead, and for the Chinese people to make great achievements. What makes it "new"? What makes it "great"? For the Chinese people, the superlative of "new" is "unprecedented", while that of "great" is "unmatched". From our long history to the vast expanse of space and time, and from planning for the well-being of the people to our role in the global community, our new era is a time of breaking through reality's limitations and opening up a bright future for our nation and the world that surpasses our imagination.

This is an era that writes a new chapter in our cause. Each generation has its own set of historical encounters and corresponding responsibilities. Socialism is a long-standing cause that requires the continuous efforts of several, dozen, or even dozens of generations. In the process of laying the foundation for socialism with Chinese characteristics, our predecessors overcame obstacles, broke through barriers, reformed the old, and created their own path towards socialism. Step by step, they created their own immortal legacy where there was once no path to follow. In the new era, socialism with Chinese characteristics stands at a historical starting point to continue building

---

A Compendium of Knowledge

The Future of New China

Published in 1902, The Future of New China is a novel written by Liang Qichao that prophesies China's prosperity and strength in 60 years' time (i.e., 1962). Liang predicts that all industries will flourish, all nations will come to China, constitutional monarchy will be established, and China will become an important pole in the international political landscape.

The New Era

The New Era is a science fiction novel written by Jin Zuoli, a late Qing Dynasty writer, and published in 1908. The story is set in 1999, at the end of the 20th century, when China has transitioned to a constitutional political system and become the world's leading power, having regained all territories that had been leased by other powerful countries.

The New China

The New China is a novel written by Lu Shi'e, a late Qing Dynasty writer, and published in 1910. The protagonist's travels to Shanghai in 1951 allow him to envision a China that has regained its leased territories and has become a world leader in terms of economic strength, military might, manufacturing capacity, and education.

upon the past and opening up new possibilities for the future. Under the new historical conditions, it is the duty of the current generation of Chinese Communists to achieve the great victory of socialism with Chinese characteristics and create a historical undertaking that meets the expectations of our forefathers and becomes beneficial for future generations.

This is an era that embarks on a new journey to build a stronger nation. In the marathon process of human transformation of the world, "modernization" has emerged as a necessary path to civilization for different peoples, regions, and

An intelligent automobile production workshop

Paper-thin "tearable" steel

Digital eco-pavilion

High-precision Liquid Crystal Display (LCD)

countries for over 200 years since the mid-18th century. So far, it has brought over 30 countries and approximately 1 billion people into the ranks of developed countries. The example set by Chinese modernization has shattered the myth that "modernization is Westernization", rendering the once-popular "blackboard economics" irrelevant, exposing various prejudices and dogmas in their original form, and inspiring other countries to explore the path of modernization with confidence, courage, and practical reference. In the new era, China is determined to build a moderately prosperous society and a modern socialist country, which gives the Chinese path to modernization new theoretical connotations and practical characteristics. This forges a new peak of human civilization, paves the way for the Chinese nation to become truly strong, and provides a new option for developing countries to achieve self-improvement.

This is an era that fulfills the new aspirations of the people. In his vision for a new social order, Marx argued that social production in the future should aim at prosperity for all. Similarly, at the inception of the People's Republic of China, Mao Zedong also proclaimed that this wealth is collective, this strength is shared, and everyone has a stake in it. Today, the Chinese people have achieved a high standard of living and are generally enjoying a moderately prosperous life. However, the uneven development among different regions and social groups persists, creating a "gap" that impedes economic and social progress. To bridge this gap and continue to meet people's aspirations for a better life, we must ensure that the benefits of economic growth are distributed more equitably through well-designed institutions. By harnessing the collective power of hundreds of millions of people, we can make significant and tangible progress towards achieving common prosperity.

This is an era that opens a new stage of aspirations. As a nation that bears deep scars of humiliation, suffering, and cultural degradation, China has an ardent and profound yearning for national rejuvenation. Following the Sino-Japanese War of 1894–1895, the *New York Times* published an article describing the Qing Dynasty as a "filthy and ugly" anachronism. This disparaging remark stung the hearts of countless Chinese people. For over a century, in order to change the destiny, the Chinese people have been steadfastly pursuing the dream of national revitalization, and the Chinese Communists, with their resolute determination of "offering my body and soul as a sacrifice for the people" and unwavering belief that "the east wind will blow again", have led the Chinese nation to a great turnaround in its destiny, achieving a magnificent transformation from an "error of the era" to an "era of China" The new era is a dawn of hope for the rejuvenation dream that is within reach, and it requires all Chinese people to work together tirelessly to fulfill the great dream and to showcase the moment of glory when the Chinese nation stands atop the pinnacle of civilization.

This is an era that demonstrates the new responsibilities of a major country. In the face of a complex and profound restructuring of the global order, contemporary China has assumed a pivotal position as a major power and

The Beijing Winter Olympics Opening Ceremony

bearer of international responsibility. Confronted with endless challenges and mounting risks on the global stage, the CPC, standing at the forefront of the global trend, has committed itself to promoting the building of a community of shared future for mankind and has conscientiously taken on the lofty responsibility of advancing progress for humanity and creating a harmonious world for all. As China enters the new era, it sends a resounding message to the world that it is ready to become a new "server" in the global development network, capable of acting as a "guardian angel" for the peaceful development of the world and poised to make even greater contributions to a brighter future for mankind.

3. Significance Marked by the New Era

Over 160 years ago, Marx analyzed the Chinese and European revolutions through the lens of the "two poles connected" law and advanced the theory of the mutual influence between China and the world. By tracing these historical threads, we can discern that the birth of the People's Republic of China coincided with the rise of national liberation movements worldwide, the launch of China's reform and opening up occurred during a period when peace and development had become the global theme, and the dawn of the new era of China emerged amidst a shifting balance of powers, with the East ascendant and the West in decline. In this sense, contemporary Chinese Communists are not only chronicling the "brief history of the future" of China, but also revising the "global history" of a great epoch in the world.

The new era marks a new leap in national rejuvenation. As China inches closer to its goal of national rejuvenation, the risks and challenges associated with this pursuit have intensified. A decade ago, amidst the fallout of the international financial crisis and the difficulties of domestic reform and development, various theories, such as Lewis' turning point, Thucydides' trap, and Tacitus' trap, emerged. These theories, along with the "China threat theory", "China collapse theory", and "China stagnation theory", were heard everywhere. Many people were watching to see how the CPC would lead the people to cross the turning point and achieve its great goals. Ten years have passed, and our steps towards national rejuvenation have not faltered; rather, they have gained momentum. Today, even those who once viewed China with skepticism are compelled to acknowledge the undeniable facts and admit, "I can't understand it, but I'm greatly impressed." Similarly, those who once harbored prejudices towards the East are forced to reassess their views and look upon China with admiration and envy, given its remarkable achievements.

The new era represents a new peak of socialism. Since the inception of the "utopia" in the early 16th century, the world has witnessed the ups and downs of socialism for over five hundred years. In China, the spark of truth ignited

---

A Compendium of Knowledge

Lewis Turning Point

The Lewis turning point is an economic concept proposed by William Arthur Lewis, a professor at the University of Manchester in England, which refers to the turning point at which a surplus of labor becomes a shortage. During the process of industrialization, as the rural labor force is gradually transferred to non-agricultural industries, the surplus rural labor force shifts from a gradual decrease to a shortage and ultimately reaches a bottleneck state.

Thucydides' Trap

The Thucydides' Trap, proposed by Harvard University professor Graham Allison, derives from the ancient Greek historian Thucydides' conclusion about the Peloponnesian War. Thucydides observed that the rise of Athens created fear in Sparta and led to inevitable conflict. Allison uses this concept to illustrate that an emerging power will inevitably challenge the position of the established power, and the established power will take measures to contain and suppress it, making conflict and even war between the two inevitable.

Tacitus Trap

The Tacitus Trap, named after Tacitus, a historian of the ancient Roman era, originally referred to a social phenomenon in which a government department or an organization loses credibility, and regardless of whether it tells the truth or lies, or engages in good or bad deeds, it is always in danger of being seen as untrustworthy.

in the early 20th century, and socialism has persevered through a century of hardships. Taking this broad historical perspective, one can better appreciate the CPC's ambitious vision of creating an ideal society for mankind. Indeed, China has revitalized socialism, and the noblest and most righteous cause of humanity has surged forward like a great river in the East after experiencing several cycles of highs and lows, reaching unprecedented new heights.

The new era points to a new direction for the world. From the history of world civilization development, the ability to "radiate" prosperity and civilization is an important indicator for measuring a country's contribution to humanity. Today, humanity is at a new crossroads in development and progress. Where is the world going? In this regard, China's remarkable achievements and ideas have been instrumental in supporting global development and influencing the world's direction, amidst the overlapping impact of the pandemic and the changes of the century. In the face of the diminishing efficacy and even side effects of the Western "miracle drugs", the magic and allure of Chinese path have captivated the world's attention as the country redefines development and progress in the new era. Its powerful magnetism is attracting an increasing number of developing countries, as if it were their destiny, to embark on the journey to the East.

Great dramas are often characterized by a series of climactic peaks. The past decade of the new era has been nothing short of historic events, but the future will be even more magnificent and thrilling. Across over 9.6 million square kilometers of land, we can expect to witness more historic miracles, as the lives of more than 1.4 billion Chinese people undergo further transformative changes. The impact of China in the 21st century will be even deeper and more far-reaching, shaping the course of history around the globe. This is our new era, and with a promising future ahead, the world awaits with bated breath.

Chapter VII

Every Majestic Mountain Range Boasts A Primary Peak

— Why are the "Two Affirmations" of decisive significance?

"Go ask the enlightened land, and go ask the thawed rivers": What has been "awakening China"? What has been driving its resurgence and flourishing? Although the mountains and rivers remain silent, the heavens and the earth bear witness to the boundless energy and vitality that courses through this land. If we explore the "source of the Great Way" – *The Book of Changes* (Zhōu Yì) – and "observe the changes of the universe to understand the changes of time; observe the customs of society to achieve the harmony of the world", as is suggested in the book, we will realize that just as great sound is imperceptible and great form is intangible, everything is self-evident and self-explanatory. Standing atop the peak of the times and listening to the divine sound, one will find that the changes and progress of the new era are all attributed to the guiding force that continues to reshape our world and the transformative ideas that illuminate our path forward.

A great era is characterized by the emergence of great figures and the birth of great ideas. In the new era, China has scored historic achievements and gone through historic changes deserving to go down in history. These historic achievements and changes are fundamentally attributed to the strong leadership of the Party Central Committee with Xi Jinping at its core, and the guiding role of Xi Jinping Thought on Socialism with Chinese Characteristics for a New Era. The Sixth Plenary Session of the 19th CPC Central Committee made it clear that the Part has established Xi Jinping's core position on the Party Central Committee and in the Party as a whole and defined the guiding role of Xi Jinping Thought on Socialism with Chinese Characteristics for a New Era. This reflects the common will of the Party, the armed forces, and Chinese people of all ethnic groups, and is of decisive significance for advancing the cause of the Party and the country in the new era and for driving forward the historic process of national rejuvenation.

1. Needs of Times, Choice of History

The relationship between great figures and the people has been a socio-historical topic of endless debate among ancient and modern thinkers. On the basis of criticizing the previous heroic view of history, Historical Materialism has correctly positioned the relationship between the two, highly affirming the main role of the people in creating history while highlighting the leading role of great figures in the activities of the masses. In the course of social development driven by the people, great figures, with their exceptional historical insight, ideological leadership, and political organization, play an irreplaceable and crucial role in the historical process. As Engels praised of Marx, "Marx stood higher, saw further, and took a wider and a quicker view than all the rest of us"; "Whatever we all are, we are through him"; "Without him we should still be stuck in the mire of confusion".

The Marxist political party is a political organization that represents the interests of the proletariat, and it is not merely an "accidental amalgamation of individuals", but a closely united entity bound by sound theories, advanced programs, and strict discipline. Among these, the central role of the party leaders and their ideas is crucial, without which the party would be reduced to a loose club, and the challenging revolutionary struggle it must undertake would be impossible to wage. Therefore, Marxist revolutionary mentors have

The Zunyi Conference (oil painting)

The venue of the Seventh National Congress of the CPC

always stressed the critical importance of maintaining the authority of the leader and their ideological position as the "lifeline" to the survival of Marxist political parties.

The CPC was established as a unified whole according to democratic centralism, but it took a long period for the Party to recognize the importance of maintaining the core of party leadership and upholding the party's ideological banner conscientiously. During the early stages of exploring the revolution, the Party leaders simply parroted "formulas" and "models" to address China's realistic problems. This approach resulted in the Chinese revolution receiving a failing grade, as the Party failed to deliver satisfactory answers. The Chinese revolution urgently needed wise leaders and effective truths. The Zunyi Conference in 1935 confirmed Mao Zedong as the de facto leader of the Central Committee and the Red Army, and saved the Party, the Red Army, and the Chinese revolution at a moment of greatest peril. At the Seventh National Congress in 1945, Mao Zedong Thought was established as the guiding philosophy of the Party, and as a result the Party became united as never before in ideological, political, and organizational terms. Although there were interruptions in the historical progress of the Chinese Revolution, such as Zhang Guotao's "setting up another Central Committee" and Wang Ming's "scrambling for power", they did not affect the significant historical status and role of Mao Zedong and Mao Zedong Thought.

This is a period of peace, yet the challenges we face, the intensity of our struggles, the difficulty of unifying our ideas, are no less and even more severe than that during the revolutionary times. At present, the rejuvenation of the Chinese nation has entered a critical period. Our goals are clear, but the obstacles ahead are beyond imagination. China is embarking on the Long March of the new era amid an unprecedentedly complex environment: the pursuit of national rejuvenation amid global changes, intertwined new contradictions and old problems, rotating tangible struggles and invisible battles, and the following foreseeable risks and unforeseeable challenges, etc. The more ambitious the goal, the more turbulent and windier the voyage, and the more essential it is to have a leading core to steer the rudder and a scientific theory to guide the navigation. Over the past decade, we have come to realize that General Secretary Xi Jinping is the most solid and reliable backbone of the Party and the Chinese people in this new era. Xi Jinping Thought on Socialism with Chinese Characteristics for a New Era is the most scientifically correct compass for the great ship of China to cleave the waves.

It was based on the profound insights of theory, the lessons of history, and the urgent needs of reality that the Party made the decisive and significant political judgment of affirming Xi Jinping's core position on the Party Central Committee and in the Party as a whole and affirming the guiding role of *Xi Jinping Thought on Socialism with Chinese Characteristics for a New Era*. This represents a thorough review of the inevitable logic and objective laws that link history and reality, as well as a profound revelation of the most fundamental guarantee for the Communist Party of China, the Chinese people, and the Chinese nation to achieve a more glorious future.

2. Shared Aspirations of the People

The key moment of history becomes eternal because of its value and significance. On November 15, 2012, Xi Jinping, as newly elected General Secretary of the CPC Central Committee, expressed his philosophy of governance: "The aspiration of the people to live a better life is the focus of our efforts." This represents the deep commitment and profound responsibility of a leader of a large political party and a major country to the people and signifies the noble pursuit of the Party Central Committee with Xi Jinping as the core in the theory and practice of governance.

From here, we see that the people's leader is always with the people. General Secretary Xi Jinping's love for the people is so deep and selfless that he states: "The concerns of the people are what I always care about, and the aspiration of the people are what I always strive for", which is a practical demonstration of his commitment to putting the people in the first place. As he once pointed out, "those who hold the people in their hearts will be held in the hearts of the people." The people's deep trust in General Secretary Xi Jinping, and

Minning Town, Ningxia

Shibadong Village, Hunan

their heartfelt support, have been expressed in simple yet warm letters sent to Zhongnanhai, expressing their deep feelings of support.

Over the past decade, numerous scenes have brought people to tears, countless words have warmed their hearts, numerous images have moved them deeply, and countless details have remained unforgettable. Let us revisit some of these moments to truly appreciate how much "the people's leader loves the people, and the people love the people's leader".

For thousands of years, the Chinese people were afflicted by poverty, but they have finally achieved their dream. In the "great fight" against poverty, General Secretary Xi Jinping braved harsh weather conditions, traveled through mud and ravines, and faced strong winds and heavy rain, visiting the poor in every corner of the country. He visited the Loess Plateau and the Qinghai-Tibet Plateau, and traveled from the Taihang Mountains to the Wumeng Mountains, from areas experiencing temperatures below freezing to areas thousands of meters above sea level. He even visited the poverty-stricken Dingxi City of Gansu and hiked across Daliang Mountain in Sichuan. Throughout his travels, he listened to the people's concerns, assessed their needs, and developed pragmatic solutions, using a series of scientific concepts and initiatives to lead the way in this monumental people's war, ultimately achieving a resounding victory.

When the lives of the common people are at stake, true valor is revealed in the flames of crisis. In the "great test" of combating Covid-19, people witnessed a strong backbone standing tall. With the epidemic putting people's lives and safety in danger, General Secretary Xi Jinping's farsighted decision-making, decisive orders, timely deployment, and unwavering determination have prioritized the protection of people's lives and health, leaving no stone unturned in the pursuit of hope. From a baby born just over 30 hours ago to an old man over 100 years old, from foreign students in China to foreign nationals residing in the country, every life has been safeguarded with utmost effort. Many have marveled at the unprecedented speed and efficacy of China's pandemic control measures, the low infection rate, and the intensity of treatment, all achieved in a country with a population of over 1.4 billion people, under the strong leadership of the Party Central Committee, with Xi Jinping at its core.

Everything about the people's interests is always a top priority. In solving the "great issue" of ensuring and improving people's wellbeing, General Secretary Xi Jinping has consistently demonstrated a deep concern for the difficulties faced by ordinary people. He prioritizes the safety and well-being of the people, sparing no effort to help them solve their problems. He resolutely practiced the principle that "lucid waters and lush mountains are invaluable assets" and adhered to the principle that "housing is for living in, not for speculation". He firmly prevented capital from competing with the people for profits and engaging in disorderly expansion and ensured that people see fairness and justice in every judicial case. He decisively implemented the "double reduction" campaign to ease the burden of excessive homework and

**Asian elephants in Yunnan Province return from their
northbound trip**

off-campus tutoring for students undergoing compulsory education and took strong measures to regulate the chaos in the entertainment industry and promote a healthy social atmosphere. Through all these efforts, General Secretary Xi Jinping demonstrates his steadfast commitment to ensuring the people are brimming with a greater sense of fulfillment, happiness, and security.

What we remember constantly will surely echo back. It is evident that General Secretary Xi Jinping's remarkable leadership, noble character, and sincere concern for the people have taken deep roots in the heart of the people. Xi Jinping Thought on Socialism with Chinese Characteristics for a New Era has manifested an extraordinary potency, one that combines the power of truth, mindset, and practice. This is the most compelling and vivid interpretation of the decisive significance of establishing Xi Jinping's core position on the Party Central Committee and in the Party as a whole and establishing the guiding role of Xi Jinping Thought on Socialism with Chinese Characteristics for a New Era.

3. Infusing It into Soul and Putting It into Action

To be at the forefront of the times, a nation must have the guidance of great leaders and the direction of advanced ideas. In realizing national rejuvenation and building China into a strong socialist country, "Two Affirmations", like a towering peak and a flying flag, inspires the nation with a long-standing civilization to undertake the great endeavor in human history.

The song "Navigating" sweeping the country

The power of great people and their ideas, once transformed into the conscious efforts of hundreds of millions of people, can converge the trickle of streams into a surging torrent, and the droplets of water into a powerful surge, unleashing the earth-shattering force to transform the land and rejuvenate the mountains and rivers. The "Two Affirmations" aims to achieve this transformation, uniting over 95 million Party members and more than 1.4 billion Chinese people – akin to sunflower seeds sticking tightly together with hearts set on the sun – to follow the leadership closely and march boldly toward the bright and glorious grand goal with unwavering determination and perseverance.

In terms of politics, it is essential to remain loyal and wholehearted. "The highest virtue in the world is loyalty." Political loyalty is the foremost quality for Party members and officials. Supporting the "Two Affirmations" requires first and foremost being loyal and supportive to General Secretary Xi Jinping, and to Xi Jinping Thought on Socialism with Chinese Characteristics for a New Era. This unwavering loyalty must always persist through any circumstance. Political loyalty is specific and unique, not abstract or general. All Party members should embody their support for the "Two Affirmations" in their ideals and convictions, political life and stances, and commitment and actions. They should also strengthen their "Four Consciousnesses", enhance their "Four-sphere Confidence", and firmly maintain the "Two Upholds", truly being loyal to the core, supporting and safeguarding it at all times.

In terms of ideology, it is crucial to be sharp-eyed and clear-hearted. Theoretical sobriety is the foundation of political firmness. "Two Affirmations" has its specific and unified political connotations. In present-day China, the sole core of the Party is General Secretary Xi Jinping. Affirming the core of the Party means affirming Xi Jinping's core position on the Party Central Committee and in the Party as a whole. Affirming the guiding position of Xi Jinping Thought on Socialism with Chinese Characteristics for a New Era means clarifying that this thought has achieved a new breakthrough in adapting Marxism to the Chinese context. It is the scientific guide and program of action for upholding and developing socialism with Chinese characteristics in the new era, as well as achieving the rejuvenation of the Chinese nation.

In terms of emotions, it is vital to be pure and sincere. Lenin once said, "without 'human emotions', there would never have been and never will be a pursuit of truth by human beings." Supporting the "Two Affirmations" means transitioning from theoretical consciousness to emotional spontaneity, from apparent consciousness to subconsciousness. It should be built upon the profound emotional foundation of genuine admiration, love, loyalty, trust, and maintenance of the Party's core from the bottom of one's heart, and upon the pursuit of truth through Xi Jinping Thought on Socialism with Chinese Characteristics for a New Era, achieving a state of "using it daily without being aware of it".

In terms of action, it is utmost to act in accordance with the requirements.

Simple Words with Deep Meaning

Quots from President Xi Jinping

Every person is remarkable.

We are all running very hard. We are all dream chasers.

We roll up our sleeves to work harder.

Officials at various levels have also spared no efforts performing their duty.

I would like to salute our great people.

Happiness is achieved through hard work.

Button the first button in their lifetime.

The country and the nation can only be good if every household lives well.

Put all your energy into ensuring a better life for the people.

Run hard on the track of youth, striving for the best performance of contemporary youth.

Actions speak louder than words. Resolutely supporting the "Two Affirmations" means that all actions should follow the guidance of General Secretary Xi Jinping and the Party Central Committee. It means truly learning, understanding, believing, and using Xi Jinping Thought on Socialism with Chinese Characteristics for a New Era. It means implementing General Secretary Xi Jinping's instructions and requirements, as well as the spirit of the Party Central Committee, to plan major strategies, develop major policies, deploy major tasks, and promote major work. It also means continuously improving the ability and level of implementation, effectively translating them into the great practice of promoting the development of the Party and the country in the new era.

Every social era calls for its own great figure, and if one does not exist, it must be created. General Secretary Xi Jinping is the great figure summoned by this era. His strength leads the course of China's destiny, and his ideas set the direction of historical progress. Under the strong leadership of the Party Central Committee, with Xi Jinping at its core, all Party members, the armed forces, and all Chinese people are filled with confidence and enthusiasm, moving towards an ever brighter and promising future.

Chapter VIII

The Banner of Thought, the Essence of the Times

— Why has Xi Jinping Thought on Socialism with Chinese Characteristics for a New Era achieved a new leap in adapting Marxism to Chinese conditions?

Human activities can be broadly classified into two categories: thought and action. Revolutionary thought is a prerequisite for revolutionary action, just as lightning precedes thunder. Each era should have its own guiding theory for its actions. With great political wisdom and theoretical courage, the Chinese Communists, led by Xi Jinping, have developed Xi Jinping Thought on Socialism with Chinese Characteristics for a New Era, which has significantly transformed China and impacted the world. General Secretary Xi Jinping, as the core of the Party Central Committee and the Party as a whole, is the primary architect of this philosophy, playing a decisive role and making decisive contributions to its creation.

In today's world, there is no other philosophy like Xi Jinping Thought on Socialism with Chinese Characteristics for a New Era that leads epoch-making changes, addresses global issues, affects billions of people, and embodies values with universal significance for humanity. This contemporary Chinese Marxism, known as Marxism of the 21st century, illuminates the great doctrine of Marxism with original theoretical contributions, a rigorous scientific system, iconic ideological views, and values that lead to action. This achievement represents a new leap in adapting Marxism to Chinese conditions and marks a new height of theoretical innovation for the CPC.

1. A New Leap and New Sublimation

Human understanding of the world has always been characterized by the unknown exceeding the known, and it has been an eternal pursuit for thinkers throughout history and across cultures to explore the unknown through the known. Whether it is the ancient Greek sages, medieval theologians, and German classical philosophers of the West, or the Confucian sages, Buddhist monks, and Taoist scholars in the East, many thinkers believed they had

Study materials on Xi Jinping Thought on Socialism with Chinese Characteristics for a New Era

unlocked the absolute laws governing the operations of all things, and that the truth ended there. Marx and Engels criticized all metaphysics based on idealism, maintaining that everything is a process, and that Marxism depends "everywhere and at all times, on the historical conditions for the time being existing". The development of Marxism reflects the historical changes, practical development, and continuous innovation of Marx, Engels, and their successors.

The greatness of Marxism lies in the fact that it "has not ended the search for truth, but rather opened the path towards it". Marxism has remained evergreen for more than a century precisely because it has consistently explored new challenges posed by the changing times and addressed new issues faced by human society. Xi Jinping Thought on Socialism with Chinese Characteristics for a New Era is a prime example of adhering to and developing Marxism. It not only respects the legacy of its predecessors but also employs Marxism as a "telescope" and "microscope" to observe the times. Furthermore, it introduces new ideas, composing a new chapter of Marxism with a fresh logical starting point and an innovative theoretical framework.

The Thought drives the rejuvenation of the Chinese nation through historical initiative. The Chinese people have been steadfast in their pursuit of achieving national rejuvenation for over a century. Xi Jinping Thought on Socialism with Chinese Characteristics for a New Era offers a profound understanding of the

---

A Compendium of Knowledge

The Titration of Civilization

Titration is a means of quantitative analysis and a chemical experimental operation, that is, to use the quantitative reaction of two solutions to determine the content of a certain solute. The titration of civilization is a fitting metaphor for cultural integration, which was first introduced by the British historian of science and technology, Joseph Lee. It refers to the exchange and integration between Chinese and Western civilizations in this context.

past and present, connecting them with the future of national rejuvenation. The Thought serves as a historical guidepost, providing a clear direction and path for the nation's efforts. Through a series of significant scientific assertions and ideological perspectives on the correct direction, political guarantees, path selection, value orientation, and guarantee of driving force, it elevates the passion of hundreds of millions of Chinese people for national rejuvenation into a rational pursuit, formulating a systematic "Theory on the Rejuvenation of the Chinese Nation".

The Thought captures the essence of Chinese culture with high confidence. Although the doctrine of Marxism originated in the West, its essence is implicitly echoed in the cultural exchanges between the East and West – a "titration[1] of civilizations" and extraction of ideas. When Marxism was introduced into China a century ago, it activated the great civilization created by the Chinese nation over thousands of years and enabled the Chinese people to shift from passive to active. Xi Jinping Thought on Socialism with Chinese Characteristics for a New Era is deeply rooted in Chinese soil. It integrates the essence of Marxist thought with the spiritual traits of Chinese culture, drawing on the nutrients of more than 5,000 years of brilliant civilization. This enriches the spiritual world of contemporary Chinese people and injects more active spiritual power to enhance national self-confidence and self-improvement. The Thought represents the essence of Chinese culture and the Chinese spirit of the times, imbued with a strong Chinese flavor, profound Chinese sentiment, and lofty national spirit. It possesses a powerful historical penetrability, cultural influence, and spiritual appeal, making it a shining example of promoting the "Two Adapts[2]."

The Thought envisages the future of humanity with a broad vision. "Seeking to improve oneself when poor and striving to benefit the world when prosperous" has long been the lofty vision and broad perspective revered by the Chinese nation since ancient times. With China's increasing global

---

1   Titration is a means of quantitative analysis and a chemical experimental operation, that is, to use the quantitative reaction of two solutions to determine the content of a certain solute. The titration of civilization is a fitting metaphor for cultural integration, which refers to the exchange and integration between Chinese and Western civilizations in this context.

2   It refers to adapting the basic tenets of Marxism to China's specific realities and China's fine traditional culture.

influence, "the interests to be considered should be the interests of all" has become an essential element of the nation's rejuvenation, and the "pursuit of progress for the humankind and the common good for the world" has become vitally important for the CPC to "establish peace for all future generations". Xi Jinping Thought on Socialism with Chinese Characteristics for a New Era has always embodied the broad vision of "a just cause should be pursued for common good". It integrates the historical process of national rejuvenation into the great tide of human civilization progress and has advanced major concepts such as building a community with a shared future for mankind, building a new type of international relations, and promoting common values of humanity, thus contributing to global peace and progress with China's wisdom.

Xi Jinping Thought on Socialism with Chinese Characteristics for a New Era charts the grand cause of the rejuvenation of the Chinese nation amid the tumult of a hundred years, delving into the vast cultural context to uncover the nourishment of the spirit of the times, and considering the direction of

Officials and the masses study Xi Jinping Thought on Socialism with Chinese Characteristics for a New Era

human destiny on the world stage. With its unparalleled power to connect time and space, explain reality, and transform practice, the era of adapting Marxism to China's conditions has achieved a qualitative leap on the "path to truth".

2. Systematic Construction and Comprehensive Development

Any classical theory that transcends time and space and has far-reaching influence must possess certain essential and prescriptive qualities; otherwise, it will lead to debates and disagreements like "Ship of Theseus" and "Ananja Drum". Simultaneously, this theory must constantly innovate with the changes of historical conditions, cultural backgrounds, and realistic needs, or else it will inevitably fall into the historical end of "ship wrecked and drum broken". When promoting theoretical classics with the times, there are typically two forms: one is the accumulation of quantity, where the original theoretical

A Compendium of Knowledge

Ship of Theseus

The Ship of Theseus is a paradox that raises questions about the sameness of objects. It poses the question: if all the constituent elements of an object are replaced, can it still be considered the original object? Theseus, the legendary king of Athens in ancient Greek mythology, had a ship named after him. The Athenians replaced the wooden planks of the ship one by one as they decayed over time, until eventually, all the planks were replaced. The Greeks then pondered whether the ship was still the same as Theseus' original ship.

The Drum of Ananja

The Drum of Ananja is a Buddhist story that emphasizes discernment. According to the story, the Buddha once told his disciples about a man named Dasaraja who owned a drum called the Ananja drum. The drum produced a beautiful sound that could be heard from tens of miles away. After using the drum for a long time, it became damaged and was repaired several times, with each part being replaced. Was the drum still the same as the original Ananja drum?

Seminar on Learning, Publicizing, and Implementing Xi Jinping Thought on Socialism with Chinese Characteristics for a New Era

framework is improved and enriched, and the other is the overall upgrade, where a new construction breakthrough occurs beyond the original theoretical framework.

It is in this sense that Xi Jinping Thought on Socialism with Chinese Characteristics for a New Era has achieved a new sublimation in adapting Marxism to the Chinese context, representing an epoch-making scientific theoretical system. This system has gradually matured and perfected through both theoretical and practical exploration since the new era, presenting a clear and complete theoretical framework and ideological content with self-consistent logic.

The theoretical thread of the Thought runs through the "Two Always": always stay committed to the founding mission, and always uphold the ideals and convictions. It serves as the immutable aim for all the Party's endeavors over the past 100 years and represents the logical origin and fundamental purpose of the Party's theoretical innovation in the new era. The most significant theoretical aim and practical direction of Xi Jinping Thought on Socialism with Chinese Characteristics for a New Era is to better serve the happiness of the Chinese people and the rejuvenation of the Chinese nation while adhering to the ideals of communism and socialist beliefs. Understanding the fundamental thread of the "Two Always" helps us comprehend the construction basis and theoretical development of this thought.

The core content of the Thought is embodied in the "Ten Affirmations"[1]. If Xi Jinping Thought on Socialism with Chinese Characteristics for a New Era is compared to a theoretical edifice, the "Ten Affirmations" are the foundational pillars supporting the entire structure. The "Ten Affirmations" are not merely a collection of scattered ideas. Instead, they seize the most critical key points in reform, development, and stability, internal and external affairs, national defense, and governance of the Party, the country, and the military. The "Ten Affirmations" form an organic whole that is both specifically directed and generally interconnected. By understanding the "Ten Affirmations", one will have grasped the essence and basic spirit of this thought.

The Thought addresses the "Three Major Questions of our Times[2]", which serve as the motto of the current era and provide a practical expression of the inner state of our times. The "Three Major Questions of our Times" are the "three questions of the times" raised to the CPC at the historical node of the new era, as well as the "theoretical eyes" that help us understand Xi Jinping Thought on Socialism with Chinese Characteristics for a New Era. In essence, the question "what kind of socialism with Chinese characteristics we should uphold and develop in this new era" discusses the direction we are heading towards, "what kind of great modern socialist country we should build" focuses on the goal and path we are taking, and "what kind of Marxist party exercising long-term governance we should develop" probes into the power guarantee that supports our efforts. By focusing on the "Three Major Questions of our Times", one can gain a clearer understanding of the direction and practical orientation of this thought.

The main ideas of the Thought are contained in the "Achievements in Thirteen Aspects[3]". To fully comprehend a theoretical system, one needs

---

1   The core content of Xi Jinping Thought on Socialism with Chinese Characteristics for a New Era was further summarized with ten key points, which are related to the most essential feature of socialism with Chinese characteristics, the general task of developing socialism with Chinese characteristics, etc.

2   The three major issues of the times are how to uphold and develop socialism with Chinese characteristics, how to build a modern and powerful socialist country, and how to build a long-time governing political party of Marxism.

3   It profoundly summed up the historic achievements and changes in the cause of the party and the country since the 18th CPC National Congress in 13 aspects such as Party leadership, Party self-governance, economic development, etc.

Ten Affirmations

The leadership of the Communist Party of China is the defining feature of socialism with Chinese characteristics and the greatest strength of the system of socialism with Chinese characteristics, and that the Party is the highest force for political leadership. Therefore, all Party members must strengthen their consciousness of the need to maintain political integrity, think in big-picture terms, follow the leadership core, and keep in alignment with the central Party leadership; stay confident in the path, theory, system, and culture of socialism with Chinese characteristics; and uphold Xi Jinping's core position on the Party Central Committee and in the Party as a whole, and uphold the Central Committee's authority and its centralized, unified leadership.

The overarching task of upholding and developing socialism with Chinese characteristics is to realize socialist modernization and national rejuvenation, and that on the basis of completing the goal of building a moderately prosperous society in all respects, a two-step approach should be taken to build China into a great modern socialist country that is prosperous, strong, democratic, culturally advanced, harmonious, and beautiful by the middle of the 21st century, and to promote national rejuvenation through a Chinese path to modernization.

The principal contradiction facing Chinese society in the new era is that between unbalanced and inadequate development and the people's ever-growing needs for a better life, and the Party must therefore remain committed to a people-centered philosophy of development, develop whole-process people's democracy, and make more notable and substantive progress toward achieving well-rounded human development and common prosperity for all.

The integrated plan for building socialism with Chinese characteristics covers five spheres, namely economic, political, cultural, social, and ecological advancement, and that the comprehensive strategy in this regard includes four prongs, namely building a modern socialist country, deepening reform, advancing law-based governance, and strengthening Party self-governance.

The overall objectives of comprehensively deepening reform are to develop and improve the system of socialism with Chinese characteristics and to modernize China's system and capacity for governance.

The overall goal of comprehensively advancing law-based governance is to establish a system of socialist rule of law with Chinese characteristics and to build a socialist rule of law country.

Learning the Resolution

China must uphold and improve its basic socialist economic system, see that the market plays the decisive role in resource allocation and the government plays its role better, have an accurate understanding of this new stage of development, apply a new philosophy of innovative, coordinated, green, open, and shared development, accelerate efforts to foster a new pattern of development that is focused on the domestic economy but features positive interplay between domestic and international economic flows, promote high-quality development, and balance development and security imperatives.

The Party's goal for military development in the new era is to build the people's armed forces into world-class forces that obey the Party's command, that are able to fight and to win, and that maintain excellent conduct.

Major-country diplomacy with Chinese characteristics aims to serve national rejuvenation, promote human progress, and facilitate efforts to foster a new type of international relations and build a human community with a shared future.

---

to examine it from both a macroscopic and microscopic perspective. This involves understanding its thematic clues, logical base, structural framework, as well as its important ideas, views, and assertions. Through "seeing the forest" and "seeing the trees" in unity, we can gain a comprehensive understanding of the historical achievements and changes summarized in the "Achievements in Thirteen Aspects". These achievements not only demonstrate the progress made by the Party and the country since the 18th National Congress, but also represent an important breakthrough in the Party's theoretical innovation in the new era. They not only provide a practical reflection of the development of the new era but also represent a theoretical innovation of contemporary Chinese Marxism.

Full and rigorous self-governance is a policy of strategic importance for the Party, and the general requirements for Party development in the new era include making all-around efforts to strengthen the Party in political, ideological, and organizational terms and in terms of conduct and discipline, with institution building incorporated into every aspect of this process, continuing the fight against corruption, and ensuring that the political responsibility for governance over the Party is fulfilled. By engaging in great self-transformation, the Party can steer great social transformation.

The essence of epoch-making systems lies in their responsiveness to the needs of their time. Xi Jinping Thought on Socialism with Chinese Characteristics for a New Era represents the culmination of the wisdom of contemporary Chinese Communists who have closely observed, understood, and steered their era. It embodies a grand vision and profound reflection on achieving the rejuvenation of the Chinese nation on the path of socialism with Chinese characteristics.

3. Theoretical Guidance and Action Plan

Historians widely agree that around 1500 A.D., the fragmented world began to integrate, opening up a history of the fusion and conflict of diverse civilizations and ideologies. Since then, human thought has been flourishing and expanding through the exchange and competition of various systems of thought. Over the past 500 years, the competition between the socialist and capitalist ideological systems has never ceased, but overall, the capitalist ideology has been stronger than the socialist ideology. Today, the world has undergone an unprecedented transformation, and Marxism has illuminated the East with its brilliant truth, heralding a historic shift in human intellectual evolution that is favorable to socialism.

Learning the Resolution

Three Major Questions of Our Times

Xi Jinping Thought on Socialism with Chinese Characteristics for a New Era has set forth a series of original new ideas, thoughts, and strategies on national governance revolving around the major questions of our times: what kind of socialism with Chinese characteristics we should uphold and develop in this new era, what kind of great modern socialist country we should build, and what kind of Marxist party exercising long-term governance we should develop, as well as how we should go about achieving these tasks.

The TV programs on theoretical discussions: "Quotes from Xi Jinping" and "Theoretical Frontier"

In the 21st century, amidst the starry sky of human thought, Xi Jinping Thought on Socialism with Chinese Characteristics for a New Era shines brilliantly and has emerged as the most profound scientific theory in the world today. With its captivating theoretical appeal, commanding spiritual influence, and potent practical efficacy, this thought steers the Chinese nation towards achieving its rejuvenation, illuminating the path towards the revitalization of socialism, and paving the way for the advancement of human civilization.

As an ideological beacon, spiritual banner, and guidance for action, Xi Jinping Thought on Socialism with Chinese Characteristics for a New Era inspires billions of people to pursue the dream of rejuvenation. Today, as the rejuvenation of the Chinese nation enters a more challenging phase, "sailing against the wind and climbing uphill" requires not only the support of material resources and social conditions but also a guiding ideology and spiritual guidance. Xi Jinping Thought on Socialism with Chinese Characteristics for a New Era serves as the "compass" and "North Star" for the rejuvenation of the Chinese nation, imbued with powerful spiritual and material strengths that are guiding nearly one-fifth of the world's population in carrying out the most ambitious and extensive social practice in human history.

With a steadfast belief in communist ideals, reform and innovation, and inclusiveness, Xi Jinping Thought on Socialism with Chinese Characteristics for a New Era has rekindled the radiance of socialism. This thought emphasizes the adherence to socialist beliefs and communist ideals as the soul and backbone of socialism, energizing the intrinsic vitality of the socialist system through reform and innovation, and assimilating and drawing from the beneficial achievements of all civilization developments, ancient and modern, to manifest the vibrancy of socialism with Chinese characteristics. Today, socialism is thriving in China, elevating this social ideal to the top of the tide amidst the ebb and flow of history, placing this social movement at the forefront of the times amidst the vicissitudes of the world.

With its distinctive path, innovative model, and advanced values, Xi Jinping Thought on Socialism with Chinese Characteristics for a New Era has illuminated the path to national strength for developing countries. Some scholars have argued that in the historical narrative of human modernization, the past has been dominated by a zero-sum game of great powers rising and falling in turn, but Chinese modernization represents a win-win scenario of "unifying goals of self and others, thus harmonizing the world", infused with Chinese wisdom and humanistic principles. The profound wisdom on governance contained in Xi Jinping Thought on Socialism with Chinese Characteristics for a New Era serves as the "golden key" unlocking the mysteries of Chinese modernization, prompting more and more countries to reconsider and choose a new path to modernization beyond the Western model.

At the core of all history lies the history of ideas. As the 21st century enters its 23rd year, questions arise: How can an ancient nation with over 5,000 years of history achieve rejuvenation? How can a social ideal that has endured for over five centuries regain its glory? And how can a world experiencing unprecedented changes find its way out? Xi Jinping Thought on Socialism with Chinese Characteristics in the New Era has emerged as a harbinger of the times, sounding the anthem of forward movement through in-depth historical contemplation.

Chapter IX

The Country Surges with Vitality, and the Nation Rises and Flourishes

— Why do we say that the CPC and the country have made historic achievements and undergone historic changes in the new era?

Over the course of ten years, spanning more than 3600 days and 87,000 hours, the clock of time has rapidly ticked away in China, leaving deep marks on the wheels of history. The passage of time relentlessly traverses between the past and the future, bearing witness to glory and dreams. Each moment of China's new era creates miracles and writes history, achieving the "impossible" and resolving "unsolvable" problems. This vibrant epoch in history is imbued with the heroic aspirations of the great people who possess the strength and determination to overcome obstacles. It sculpts the magnificent scenes of a great nation with unprecedented splendor and inscribes the immortal poems of a great era, destined to endure between heaven and earth for eternity.

The greatness of a cause is not only measured by its brilliant accomplishments, but also by the grandeur of the process. In the new era, the Party Central

Committee with Xi Jinping at its core has demonstrated great historical initiative, tremendous political courage, and a powerful sense of mission. It has solved many tough problems that were long on the agenda but never resolved and accomplished many things that were wanted but never got done. With this, it has prompted historic achievements and historic shifts in the cause of the Party and the country. The Sixth Plenary Session of the 19th Central Committee of the Communist Party of China highlighted the remarkable achievements made by the Party and the people since the 18th National Congress from 13 aspects, unveiling a vibrant and flourishing landscape of China. Standing at the pinnacle of history and observing the road ahead, we are filled with confidence in our great cause, with boundless hope and aspirations for a better future.

1. Original Ideas Being Profound

The course of history is magnificent, and the creation of theory is vigorous. In the past decade, in creating the "greatest development miracle on earth", contemporary Chinese Communists have established Xi Jinping Thought on Socialism with Chinese Characteristics for a New Era with epoch-making practical and theoretical innovations. They have put forward a series of original, systematic, and guiding scientific assertions that have profoundly addressed the major questions of our times regarding the development of the Party and the country, achieving a new theoretical breakthrough. This new era, with a clear path and boundless achievements, is fundamentally achieved through the continuous guidance of thought and theory.

History serves as a mirror that reflects the light of truth. By looking back at the past, we can not only pick the stunning and dazzling flowers but also tap into the rushing fire of the earth. Tracing the intertwined historical trajectory of theory and practice, we explore the underlying ideological code and theoretical logic behind great achievements, search for the torch of thought, and feel the radiance of theory. In this way, we can witness how the light of truth has illuminated the grand journey of a great nation towards rejuvenation, and how the fire of wisdom has ignited the majestic power of an

The Historic Achievements and Historic Changes in Thirteen Aspects

(1) With regard to upholding the Party's overall leadership, the Party Central Committee's authority and its centralized, unified leadership have remained robust, the Party's leadership systems have improved, and the way in which the Party exercises its leadership has become more refined. There is greater unity among all Party members in terms of thinking, political resolve, and action, and the Party has significantly boosted its capacity to provide political leadership, give guidance through theory, organize the people, and inspire society.

(2) With regard to exercising full and rigorous self-governance, the Party's ability to improve and reform itself and maintain its integrity has been significantly strengthened, and the problem of lax and weak governance over Party organizations has been addressed at the fundamental level. An overwhelming victory has been achieved in the fight against corruption, and this momentum has been consolidated across the board. The Party has grown stronger through revolutionary tempering.

(3) With regard to pursuing economic development, our economic development has become much more balanced, coordinated, and sustainable. China's economic strength, scientific and technological capabilities, and composite national strength have reached new heights. Our economy is now on a path of higher-quality development that is more efficient, equitable, sustainable, and secure.

(4) With regard to deepening reform and opening up, the Party has consistently promoted broader and deeper reform across the board. The system of socialism with Chinese characteristics is now more mature and well-defined, and the modernization of China's system and capacity for governance has reached a higher level. The cause of the Party and the country now radiates with fresh vitality.

(5) With regard to advancing political work, we have actively developed whole-process people's democracy, made comprehensive sweeping progress in improving the institutions, standards, and procedures of China's socialist democracy, and given better play to the strengths of the Chinese socialist political system. As a result, our political stability, unity, and dynamism have been reinforced and grown stronger.

(6) With regard to comprehensively advancing law-based governance, the system of socialist rule of law with Chinese characteristics has constantly been improved, solid progress has been made in advancing the rule of law in China, and the Party's ability to lead and govern the country through law-based methods has been notably enhanced.

(7) With regard to cultural advancement, we have seen a sweeping and fundamental shift in the ideological domain, a notable boost in confidence in our culture among all Party members and all Chinese people, and a major increase in cohesiveness throughout society. All of this has provided solid ideological guarantees and powerful inspiration for opening up new horizons for the cause of the Party and the country in the new era.

(8) With regard to promoting social advancement, the people's lives have improved in all areas, public participation in social governance is growing, and social governance is becoming smarter, more law-based, and more specialized. We have continued to develop a sound atmosphere in which people are able to live and work in peace and contentment and social stability and order prevail. As a result, China's miracle of long-term social stability has continued.

(9) With regard to spurring ecological advancement, the Central Committee has devoted greater efforts than ever before to ecological conservation and made significant progress in building a Beautiful China. Our environmental protection endeavors have seen sweeping, historic, and transformative changes.

(10) With regard to strengthening national defense and the armed forces, the people's military has been through an all-around revolutionary restructuring in preparation for the next stage, while our defense capabilities have grown in step with our economic strength. Firmly carrying out the missions of the new era, the people's military has taken concrete actions to safeguard our national sovereignty, security, and development interests with an indomitable fighting spirit.

(11) With regard to safeguarding national security, we have enhanced security on all fronts and overcome many political, economic, ideological, and natural risks, challenges, and trials. This has helped ensure that the Party and the country thrive and enjoy lasting stability.

(12) With regard to upholding the policy of One Country, Two Systems and promoting national reunification, the Central Committee has adopted a series of measures to address both symptoms and root causes of relevant issues. It has ensured resolute implementation of the principle of patriots governing Hong Kong and Macao. These moves have helped to restore order in Hong Kong and ensure a turn for the better in the region. All this has laid a solid foundation for advancing law-based governance in Hong Kong and Macao and for securing steady and continued success of the One Country, Two Systems policy. Upholding the one-China principle and the 1992 Consensus, we firmly oppose separatist activities seeking "Taiwan independence" and firmly oppose foreign interference. We have maintained the initiative and the ability to steer in cross-Strait relations.

(13) With regard to bolstering the diplomatic front, we have advanced major-country diplomacy with Chinese characteristics on all fronts. The concept of a human community with a shared future has become a banner leading trends of the times and human progress. China has broken new ground in its diplomatic endeavors amid profound global changes and turned crises into opportunities amid complex situations on the international stage. These efforts have resulted in a marked increase in China's international influence, appeal, and power to shape.

Eastern country to influence the world.

It has greatly enriched classical theory. Marxism, which emerged over 170 years ago, is like a majestic sunrise that illuminates the bright path for human beings to achieve their own liberation. We are still in the historical era indicated by Marxism, and what we need to do is to further carry forward this theory and radiate the clear light of profound thought. Xi Jinping Thought on Socialism with Chinese Characteristics for a New Era combines adherence and development, "returning to Marxist classics" without "sticking to Marxist classics". Based on the requirements of the new era and practical development, it has put forward many new perspectives that predecessors have not discussed, greatly enriching the treasury of Marxist classics.

It has drawn profound nourishment from history. "The past is not as fleeting as smoke." While history may have dissipated like smoke and vanished with the wind in terms of social existence, it has left a lasting impact on social consciousness. Today's China has emerged from the depths of history, with the refined essence of its civilization profoundly shaping the unique spiritual temperament of the Chinese nation. With a profound understanding of historical perspectives, Xi Jinping Thought on Socialism with Chinese Characteristics for a New Era penetrates the countless changes in Chinese civilization over 5000 years, examines the vicissitudes of the past 180 years of China's modern history, and reflects on the successes and failures of the CPC over the past century. This approach draws wisdom and inspiration from the depths of history, enhancing the explanatory power and appeal of theory in the new era.

It has scientifically summarized practical experience. The era is the origin of thought, and practice is the source of theory. The more vibrant the social practice, the more explosive the emergence of ideas and theories. In the face of unprecedented "big" factors such as the global transformation, the pandemic of the century, China's tremendous changes, and its national rejuvenation, there is an urgent need to find explanations and effective governance strategies. Xi Jinping Thought on Socialism with Chinese Characteristics for a New Era is based on the great practices of contemporary China and the world. Taking ongoing events as examples and ongoing undertakings as its focus, it derives from practice, adheres to practice as the criterion, and aims to guide Chinese practice with Chinese theories and use Eastern wisdom to address global challenges.

2. Transformative Practices Truly Remarkable

Throughout the evolution of the universe and the vicissitudes of human affairs, change is an eternal law. Examining the changes in human history, adapting to changing circumstances and embracing new trends at specific historical junctures have been the winning strategies for a nation or a country to rise to a higher level. Since the beginning of the new era, our domestic and international environments have undergone profound and complex changes, with new situations and problems constantly emerging, and new contradictions and challenges arising one after another. It is at this critical moment, like a river entering a gorge or a gust of wind passing through

---

A Record of History Today

Reforming Government Functions

It refers to reforms to delegate power, streamline administration, and optimize government services. "Delegate power" can lower the threshold for access; "streamline administration" means developing new ways of regulation and supervision to promote fair competition; and "optimize government services" refers to providing efficient services to create a favorable environment. This initiative has been instrumental in deepening administrative system reform and transforming government functions since the 18th National Congress of the Communist Party of China. The accompanying image shows police officers in Taizhou City, Zhejiang Province, strictly implementing the requirements of the reform to provide better public service "without the need for a second visit".

| A Record of History Today |

Reform of Rural Land System

Reform of rural land system is a critical aspect of deepening rural reform since the 18th National Congress. Its main task is to orderly promote reforms of rural collective construction land for commercial use, rural homesteads, and land expropriation system. In December 2014, the General Office of the CPC Central Committee and the General Office of the State Council issued the "Opinions on the Pilot Reforms of rural land expropriation, Collective Construction Land for Commercial Use Entering the Market, and Homesteads System". Since then, rural land system reforms have been gradually promoted across the country. The accompanying image depicts farmers in Rongjiang County, Guizhou Province, receiving their rural land contract management right certificates.

a narrow pass, that decisive actions are needed. Standing at the historical juncture of the crucial leap for national rejuvenation, it is urgent to cultivate new opportunities amidst crises, open up new possibilities through changes, and achieve systemic reforms to upgrade our power. This will help steer the "China Ship" through turbulent waters, break through the "island chain" of problems, navigate through the "vortex of contradictions", and sail smoothly towards new horizons at full speed.

In the new era, the Party Central Committee with Xi Jinping at its core has seized the opportunity and steadfastly sounded the clarion call for a renewed wave of reforms. In the great process of comprehensively deepening reform, the two Decisions[1] of the third plenary session of the 18th Central Committee and the fourth plenary session of the 19th Central Committee have consistently provided a clear roadmap for "China's changes" and "China's governance". This roadmap charts a grand blueprint for upholding and improving the socialist system with Chinese characteristics, advancing the

---

1   The Decision on Some Major Issues Concerning Comprehensively Deepening Reforms in 2013, and the Decision on Some Major Issues Concerning How to Uphold and Improve the System of Socialism with Chinese Characteristics and Advance the Modernization of China's System and Capacity for Governance in 2019.

modernization of China's system and capacity for governance, thereby laying a solid institutional foundation for achieving national rejuvenation.

In terms of "coverage", the reform spans all areas and sectors. Since the third plenary session of the 11th Central Committee, China has embarked on a gradual path of reform, extending from rural to urban areas, from outside to inside the system, and from the economic field to other areas, unfolding step by step. At this stage of reform, its interconnectedness, coupling and systemic nature have become increasingly prominent, requiring a comprehensive, systematic approach rather than piecemeal efforts. Since the 18th National Congress, the comprehensive deepening of reform has been focused on overall planning and strategic arrangements. Over 2,000 measures have been introduced, covering various aspects and fields such as the economy, politics, culture, society, ecological civilization, and Party development. These reforms have driven comprehensive efforts, multiple breakthroughs, steady progress, and in-depth advancement. They have laid solid foundations, established essential institutional framework in various fields, and achieved historic changes, systematic reshaping, and overall reconstruction in many areas. It can be said that over the past decade, the reform has blossomed comprehensively and flourished in various sectors, forming a vibrant picture of reform and opening up in the new era.

In terms of "breakthroughs", the reform has dared to tackle tough challenges and navigate through treacherous rapids. It can be said that the easy and universally welcomed reforms have been completed, and the delicious meat has already been consumed. What remains are the hard bones to be gnawed and the rocky shoals to be traversed. Wherever these hard bones and rocky shoals exist, they represent areas with ideological shackles, institutional barriers, and deeply entrenched interests that have solidified over time. Such obstacles are not the result of a single day's effort, and breaking through them requires persistent efforts and a systematic approach. Since the 18th National Congress, the comprehensive deepening of reform has directly targeted key areas and essential issues, confronting the core contradictions and addressing vested interested. They have successfully resolved longstanding "tough nuts to

A Record of History Today

Deepening Judicial System Reform

Deepening the judicial system reform to develop a fair, efficient, and authoritative socialist judicial system is important for modernizing China's system and capacity for governance. The third and fourth plenary sessions of the 18th Central Committee made significant decisions and plans to deepen the reform of the judicial system. They proposed a series of major reform initiatives, such as promoting four pilot reforms centered on the judicial accountability system, improving the supporting system for basic reforms, such as the post system for judges, advancing litigation procedure system and trial mechanism reform, actively promoting the organizational reform of people's courts, and steadily advancing the pilot reform of the people's assessor system. At the 19th CPC National Congress, the task of deepening the comprehensive and complementary reform of the judicial system was put forward. The picture shows the whole-process mobile case handling system launched by the construction of a smart court in Shenzhen Intermediate People's Court, Guangdong Province.

crack" that had accumulated over many years and effectively cured the "chronic ailments" that had long plagued development of various endeavors.

In terms of "implementation", the reform has persistently smashed away at obstacles with determination. Reform inevitably involves deep-level adjustment of interests. Just as "those whose cheese is moved will oppose it", those who stand to lose from such adjustments may also resist changes. The difficulties and resistance to change will increase as reforms progress, necessitating a resolute focus on implementation with repeated efforts. General Secretary Xi Jinping has taken a hands-on approach to reform, personally leading, deploying, and supervising the implementation, and convening meetings intensively to ensure effective implementation. Each initiative is pushed forward step by step, each matter is attended to one by one, and each milestone is carefully monitored to ensure progress. This resolute approach has left a lasting mark of tenacity, paving the way for the

A Record of History Today

The Adjustment of Family Planning Policy

In an effort to improve China's population structure and promote long-term balanced population development, China has gradually adjusted its family planning policy since the 18th CPC National Congress. On December 21, 2013, the CPC Central Committee and the State Council issued the "Opinions on Adjusting and Improving Birth Policies", which proposed the two-child policy for couples of which one partner is an only child. On December 31, 2015, the CPC Central Committee and the State Council made a "Decision on Implementing a Universal Two-Child Policy and Reforming and Improving Family Planning Service Management". On June 26, 2021, the CPC Central Committee and the State Council issued the "Decision on Improving Birth Policies to Promote Long-Term Balanced Population Growth", which proposed the implementation of a policy that allows for a couple to have three children and includes supporting measures. The image depicts a harmonious family with three children.

success of the reform efforts. Under the strong promotion of the Party Central Committee, countless "blockages" have been overcome, and numerous "last kilometers" have been connected. The comprehensive deepening of reforms is yielding dividends in various fields, revealing the power and vitality of the Party and the country which continue to flow and erupt.

3. Breakthroughs Being Unprecedented

In the second decade of the 21st century, the world economy has been mired in a slump following the international financial crisis, and many countries have struggled with their development – some call it a "Little Ice Age" for humanity. Despite this, China has achieved unprecedented breakthroughs in a remarkably short period of time. The scope, depth, and impact of these changes are not only historical but also global, profoundly transforming the country, the nation, and the people, and influencing the course of human development.

Indeed, when we extend the timeline and widen the spatial perspective, we can clearly see that the breakthroughs made in the past decade are unprecedented. The development in many fields is not merely a continuous accumulation at a quantitative level, but also a leapfrog advancement on a qualitative level. It involves not only the expansion of strength, extent, and scope, but also the breaking of conceptual, structural, and ideological barriers. Therefore, it can be confidently stated that the cause of the Party and the country is making significant strides forward and ascending to new heights.

This has been a decade of unprecedented growth in China's comprehensive national strength. Over the past ten years, China's national economy has grown in both quantity and quality, with a more balanced, coordinated, and sustainable economic development. The GDP has surpassed the milestone of 100 trillion yuan, and per capita GDP has exceeded $10,000, with continuous optimization in the proportions of the "three industries" and "three driving forces". The Chinese economy is running steadily in the new era. China has amazed the world with its impressive achievements in science and technology, including the Chang'e lunar exploration missions, the Tianwen-1 Mars mission, the establishment of the Chinese space station with a "permanent residence", the progress of the Xuelong-2 ice breaker in the polar regions, and the introduction of the Jiuzhang quantum computer, among other cutting-edge technologies. Maga-projects such as the Beijing Daxing International Airport, the Hong Kong-Zhuhai-Macau Bridge, and the national computing network to synergize east and west have achieved remarkable success. Moreover, China's advancements in technology, including 5G, big data, cloud computing, the Internet of things, new energy vehicles, smart phones, and industrial robots, are leading the world. Today, "Made in China", "Quality Made in China", and "Intelligent Manufacturing in China", are working together to create new miracles that will continue to impress the world.

This has been a decade of steady improvement in people's wellbeing. Over the past ten years, the overall standard of living has not only seen continuous

*Tianwen-*1 **Mars probe**

*Chang'e-*5 **lunar probe**

*Xuelong-*2 **polar research ship**

Jiuzhang **quantum computer**

Chinese Space Station

growth but has also taken significant steps towards common prosperity. Between 2012 and 2021, the national per capita disposable income increased from 16,510 yuan to 35,128 yuan, exhibiting an average annual growth rate that outperformed the economic growth rate. Moreover, the Engel coefficient of the national residents was 29.8% in 2021, meeting the affluence standard established by the United Nations. The well-being of the people has been comprehensively enhanced, with continuous improvements in the quality of life and significant increases in people's sense of fulfillment, happiness, and

A Record of History Today

National Computing Network to Synergize East and West

The national computing network to synergize east and west aims to develop a new network system that integrates cloud computing, big data, and data centers. This initiative seeks to optimize the construction of data centers and promote synergy between the eastern and western regions of China. In February 2022, China approved projects to build eight national computing hubs in the Beijing-Tianjin-Hebei region, the Yangtze River Delta, the Guangdong-Hong Kong-Macao Greater Bay Area, the Chengdu-Chongqing economic circle, Inner Mongolia, Guizhou, Gansu, and Ningxia. In addition, China has approved plans on 10 national-data center clusters, indicating the completion of the overall layout for the national integrated big-data center system and the official launch of the national computing network to synergize east and west. The attached image displays the network base in western Zhongwei City, Ningxia Hui Autonomous Region.

security. China has achieved the goal of building a moderately prosperous society in all aspects, with the size of the middle-income group reaching 400 million, absolute poverty being historically eradicated, and all people running on the path to a better life.

This has been a decade of unprecedented surge in national self-confidence. Over the past ten years, our confidence in the path, theory, system, and culture of socialism with Chinese characteristics have become the most stirring and inspiring elements of our rejuvenated nation and advancing era. Grand celebrations marking the 70th anniversary of the founding of the People's Republic of China and the 100th anniversary of the founding of the Communist Party of China have demonstrated the Chinese idea of harmony and order. International events like the Asian Cultural Carnival and the opening and closing ceremonies of the Beijing Winter Olympics and Paralympics have showcased the charm of the East and the romance of China. Masterpieces, including *The Wandering Earth* and *My People, My Country*, have also expressed great love and patriotism. The aspirations, determination, and confidence of billions of Chinese people have been greatly enhanced, resulting in an ongoing rise in self-esteem, self-confidence, and pride. This positive shift

Grand Performance of Asian Cultural Carnival

Lantern Festival in the Forbidden City

is reflected in the values of the post-1949 generation, the 1970s and 1980s generation, the Z generation Z, and the AA generation, whose mental states are now more rational and peaceful. Our nation has never been prouder and more confident as it is today, and our people have never been more energetic and optimistic as they are today.

This has been a decade of great strides in China's foreign diplomacy. Over the past ten years, China has advocated for the building of a community with a shared future for mankind, the development of a new type of international relations, and the promotion of common values for all humanity. Major events such as the APEC Beijing Summit, G20 Hangzhou Summit, BRICS Xiamen Summit, and World Political Parties Summit have showcased China's unique charm. Moreover, significant platforms like the "Belt and Road" Forum for International Cooperation, China International Import Expo, and Beijing International Fair for Trade in Services have demonstrated China's contribution to the world. China's diplomatic efforts have unfolded in a comprehensive, multi-dimensional, and three-dimensional manner, playing an increasingly vital role on the world stage. China actively participates in

---

A Compendium of Knowledge

Generation Z

Generation Z, also known as the "Net Generation", "Internet Generation", "2D Generation", and "Digital Media Indigenous", denotes a cohort of individuals born between 1995 and 2009. This group of individuals have been seamlessly connected to the Internet since birth, and have been significantly influenced by digital information technology, instant communication devices, and smart phone products.

The AA Generation

The AA Generation typically refers to those born after 2010. This generation has grown up with mobile Internet, Internet of Things, and other advanced technologies, and are highly attuned to emerging technologies and applications, such as 5G, cloud computing, artificial intelligence, and the metaverse.

The CPC and World Political Parties Summit

the reform and construction of the global governance system, taking on more and more international responsibilities in addressing climate change, reducing poverty and hunger, preventing and controlling infectious diseases, and combating terrorism. China has shown itself as a responsible major country. With the significant increase in China's international influence, appeal, and shaping power, more and more people believe that "China is the new hope for the future of the world" and assert that "the development of the world in the 21st century depends on China".

4. Landmark Achievements Impressing the World

History is often remembered for those shining moments that sparkle brilliantly. Each groundbreaking achievement, each earth-shaking event, and each monumental project form a grand narrative of historic achievements and transformative changes. They indicate the broad path of historical progress, composing the magnificent symphony of the era's transformations.

The iconic achievements of the new era, like a splendid galaxy of shining stars, illuminate the ever-changing land of China, permeating all aspects of its economic and social life, and happening right before everyone's eyes. Through concrete lenses such as "China from above", "China from high-speed rail", and "China along the expressways", we can capture and witness the breathtaking moments and magnificent scenes that shape a changing China and a nation in motion. "A glimpse reveals the whole", and among the most outstanding and remarkable achievements, a few stand out prominently, leaving a profound impact and painting a vivid picture of China's journey in the new era.

In eradicating absolute poverty, we have achieved an unprecedented victory in the largest-scale fight against poverty in human history, with concerted efforts and full commitment. Poverty has been a persistent issue throughout human history, spanning successive Chinese dynasties and remaining unresolved in many developed Western countries to this day. However, this global challenge has been thoroughly addressed by China in the new era. Since the 18th National Congress, all 832 impoverished counties have

The Mulao Ethnic Group in Luocheng, Guangxi, Achieved Overall Poverty Eradication

The Mulao is one of the ethnic minorities with a smaller population in China. Luocheng County in Guangxi Zhuang Autonomous Region is the only Mulao autonomous county in China. At the end of 2020, Luocheng Mulao autonomous county was officially removed from the list of impoverished counties, and the Mulao ethnic group achieved poverty alleviation for the entire ethnicity, forging ahead towards a better future with increasingly firm steps. As seen in the picture, the "Ten Sisters of Mulao" live streaming team from the county is promoting local agricultural and specialty products online.

shaken off poverty, all 128,000 poverty-stricken villages have been removed from the list, and nearly 100 million rural impoverished population have been lifted out of poverty. China achieved the poverty reduction target of the United Nations 2030 Agenda for Sustainable Development 10 years ahead of schedule, creating a miracle in the history of poverty reduction. Countless impoverished people have moved from destitution to a moderately prosperous life. The "Two Assurances and Three Guarantees"[1] has become a standard provision. Moreover, all 28 less populated ethnic groups have been lifted out of poverty, and the appearance of impoverished population has been completely transformed. Everywhere in the newly emerged poverty-free areas, one can observe the joyous scenes of transformation and progress. This incredible achievement will be remembered in the annals of Chinese national development and human social progress, leaving a lasting impact for generations to come.

In exercising full and rigorous Party self-governance, we have persisted and

---

1   The Two Assurances and Three Guarantees refer to assurances of adequate food and clothing, and guarantees of access to compulsory education, basic medical services and safe housing for impoverished rural residents.

A Record of History Today

Fugitives on Interpol Red Notice Captured

In October 2021, Jiang Dongmei, former deputy secretary of the Party Committee and president of Liaoyang Rural Commercial Bank in Liaoning Province, was arrested overseas and repatriated to China for prosecution.

pursued it to the end, achieving an overwhelming victory in the fight against corruption and fully consolidating the results. Corruption is not a recent problem, not is it unique to China. It is a longstanding socio-historical problem widely recognized as the "cancer of politics". Some in the West have asserted that corruption is an insoluble issue in a two-party or multi-party system, and that it is even more difficult for the CPC, which holds sole power, to reform itself. However, since the 18th CPC National Congress, the Party Central Committee with Xi Jinping as its core has fearlessly advanced the Party's self-revolution, unwaveringly pursued full and strict self-governance, and resolutely cracked down on corruption at all levels, targeting "tigers", "flies", and "foxes"[1]. According to statistics, as of October 2021, the disciplinary and supervisory agencies across the country have initiated investigations into 4.078 million cases involving 4.379 million individuals, investigated and examined 484 senior officials under the Central Committee's jurisdiction, and imposed disciplinary and administrative sanctions on 3.998 million individuals. The intensity of Party governance and the crackdown on corruption have been evaluated by some scholars as unprecedented in China's history and in global political history.

In the pursuit of building a Beautiful China, we have taken strict measures

---

1   "Tigers", "flies", and "foxes" refer to corrupted officials of different ranks.

Yucun, a village in Anji county of Zhejiang province

The Saihanba Mechanical Forest Farm in north China's Hebei province

against pollution and implemented systematic governance, bringing about historic, transformative, and comprehensive changes in ecological environment protection. During the process of industrialization and modernization, developed Western countries generally followed the path of "polluting first, cleaning up later", which seemed inevitable. China, in its middle and late stages of industrialization, faced heavy ecological and environmental costs due to long-term lax development. Since the 18th National Congress, the Party has regarded the construction of an ecological civilization as a fundamental task for the sustainable development of the Chinese nation and has taken unprecedented efforts to strengthen ecological and environmental protection with unprecedented determination, intensity, and effectiveness. Pollution prevention and control have been accelerated, and green development has entered the "fast lane". The once-polluted landscapes are now being restored, and a beautiful China with blue skies, green lands, and clear waters is increasingly visible to the world. This remarkable achievement not only has a lasting impact on the Chinese nation but also makes immeasurable contributions to our planet. According to satellite data, approximately one-fourth of the world's new greening area in recent years has come from China, ranking first in the world.

As the saying goes, "the land is so beautiful, attracting countless heroes to compete". Looking back at the past, the journey towards victory has painted a magnificent picture. Looking towards the future, the grand vision of rejuvenation presents a desirable and beautiful prospect. For those who have climbed through layers of peaks, a magnificent sunrise and sea of clouds await them with a single effort to move up one more level. Similarly, the vanguards who carry the long-cherished aspirations of generations will witness the moment when dreams come true, as long as they forge ahead and strive for another stretch.

Chapter X

A Magnificent Scroll Enduring Heaven and Earth

— What is the historical significance of the CPC's century-long endeavors?

The powerful wind blows, and the mighty tide surges. Just as the Yangtze River and the Yellow River constantly roar with vitality, the sacred fire of China's vibrant civilization has endured for thousands of years. Over the past hundred years, the Chinese nation, which has endured immense suffering, has gone through countless hardships and twists and turns under the leadership of the CPC. It has weathered the stormy nights unwaveringly, traversed the mists of the mountains, and ushered in the radiant dawn of the rejuvenation, displaying the grand momentum of the dragon of the East soaring with the wind. The past century has been a hundred years of vicissitudes, with great changes taking place. Throughout the changing scenes of history, an ideology originating from the West and a civilization rooted in the East have interwoven. The growth of a century-old political party and the rebirth of a millennium-old nation have become one, forming a stunning chapter of history on the vast land of China. This transformation has completely changed the destiny of the Chinese people, reshaped the landscape of the ancient country spanning thousands of miles, and rewritten the development pattern of human society.

In the blink of an eye, the stars have shifted; in a fleeting moment, a century has passed. The light and shadow of a century have witnessed the arduous journey and revival of a nation that has experienced countless trials, reflecting the legendary transformation of an ancient country with a long history from suffering to glory. Only by following the coordinates of time and restoring the scenes of history can we truly comprehend the meaning of history. As we contemplate the past and present, filled with emotions, let us return to the origin of history, reopen the gate of time, and follow the river of years downstream, carefully understanding the great history of the CPC's century-long endeavors and deeply appreciating the great achievements made by the Party in leading the people to create an extraordinary record in history.

1. Fundamental Changes in the Fate of the Chinese People

The Chinese people have long been known to the world for their abundant lives and civilized etiquette, standing out among nations. In ancient Greek literature, China was referred to as "Serica", meaning a nation rich in silk and imbued with warmth, happiness, and justice. In the *Travels of Marco Polo*, a glamorous and wealthy China was introduced to Europeans. The German philosopher Leibniz described China as one of the greatest and most elegant civilizations of mankind in his book *Novissima Sinica*. For thousands of years, the Chinese people have stood at the pinnacle of civilization, with the majesty of a heavenly kingdom, earning the admiration and reverence of other civilizations and nations.

However, the Chinese people embarked on their journey into modern times with a deep sense of shame. In less than a century, from the 1840s to the 1920s, Beijing, the capital of the Qing Dynasty, was twice ransacked by foreign invaders. As a result, the Chinese people found themselves "under collapsed roofs, in leaking boats, and amidst burning fires", suffering in dire circumstances, struggling on the edge of life and death. The humiliation,

The barbaric invasion by the armies of the Western powers a hundred
years ago

The National Day Parade on the 70th Anniversary of the Founding of the
People's Republic of China

hardship, and misery they experienced were unparalleled in human history. At that time, the Chinese people were like "fish at the bottom of a cauldron", vulnerable to being slaughtered. They could not even guarantee their basic safety, let alone the satisfaction of material well-being, and their personal dignity and pride were even more out of reach.

Today, after more than a century of resistance and struggle, the Chinese people have finally ushered in a major turnaround in their fate. From "being

Chinese athletes who participated in the Olympics for the first time
were disheartened

The exuberant Chinese team at the Beijing Winter Olympics

ashamed to be Chinese" to "having no regrets in being part of the Chinese nation", from "the dragon throne of the Qing dynasty becoming a prop for foreign invaders' photos" to "those who dare to offend China will be eventually punished, no matter how far they are", from looking up to the West with inferiority and weakness to confidently facing the world on equal footing … More than 1.4 billion Chinese people have risen to political, economic, and spiritual heights, basking in the infinite glory and pride of their Chinese heritage.

Invaders posing for photographs on the throne of the Qing
Emperor a century ago

Recent evacuation operations for overseas Chinese carried
out by the Chinese government

The course of history is tumultuous and erratic, illustrating the stark disparities between the nadirs and zeniths of the Chinese people's destiny. This sense of resurgence and reversal is so intense that it can only be indelibly etched in the fabric of a century of interconnected cycles of fortune, marked by both triumphs and setbacks.

A century ago, the Chinese people were weighed down by the oppressive yoke of the "Three Mountains", treated as slaves and dogs, struggling to survive even while kneeling, and humiliated by Western powers as the "Sick Man of

Old China was characterized by primitive and backward
agricultural practices

Contemporary agricultural production is characterized by large-
scale mechanization

East Asia". Today, the Chinese people stand tall and proud, having completely escaped the fate of being bullied, oppressed, and enslaved, becoming the masters of their own country, society, and destiny. They enjoy comprehensive democratic rights, wielding control over national affairs, economic and cultural enterprises, and social affairs. China has transformed into a new nation, where hundreds of millions of people have truly internalized the adage "I am the master of my own land" and "I have the final say in my own affairs".

A century ago, the old China was mired in poverty and weakness, with an overwhelming population suffering from starvation, lack of shelter, and

Chinese athletes who achieved gold medals during the Beijing Winter Olympics

displacement. Countless individuals lacked necessities like clothing and food, causing untold misery and destitution. Today, the Chinese people have achieved unprecedented prosperity, putting an end to the era of material scarcity and deprivation. The days of famine and freezing are long gone, and absolute poverty has been eradicated from China. Over 1.4 billion people have embarked on the path to overall moderate prosperity and shared wealth. The aspiration for a better life is continuously turning into reality. Today's China has undergone a profound transformation, and hundreds of millions of people are truly living a happy life of "no one left cold or hungry, and well-being is found everywhere".

A century ago, Chinese people, disparagingly referred to as "Fu Manchu" or "slant-eyed" by Westerners were dispirited and listless. They relied on opium to numb their restless souls and find temporary solace. The cartoon scene of "carrying a big duck egg on a stretcher" at the Olympic Games dealt a crushing blow to the nation's morale. Today, the Chinese people are imbued with vitality and dynamism, expressing genuine affection and confidence in their Chinese culture, history, and traditions, displaying unprecedented enthusiasm for the Party, the country, and socialism. They have consistently surpassed their own limits, setting new records at the Olympic Games, exemplifying robust physical health, as well as exhibiting civilized spirits that inspire confidence. China has now undergone a dramatic transformation, where hundreds of millions of people exude a spirited and confident demeanor.

It is a century of splendor, an epic of the people. A hundred years of struggle and perseverance has nurtured a flourishing nation, permeating the lives of every Chinese with abundant resources and prosperity. Across the land, the Chinese people have grown more self-assured, self-reliant, and self-improving, significantly bolstering their aspirations, resilience, and fortitude. The tremendous energy accumulated throughout history is fully unleashed, radiating an unprecedented historical initiative and creative spirit. With utmost confidence, they are writing the great history of China's development in the new era.

2. Successful Establishment of the Path Towards Rejuvenation

Spanning 5000 years and stretching 10,000 miles, the long scroll of Chinese history unfolds. Our ancestors once created a glorious civilization that led the world for thousands of years. According to the renowned British scholar, Angus Maddison, in his *The World Economy: A Millennial Perspective*, China's GDP accounted for more than 20% of the world's total since the 10th century AD. However, this great empire and glorious nation suffered a decline in the drastic changes of modern world history, falling into the tragic abyss of "assessing China's existing national strength and trying to satisfy foreign invaders under the premise of what it can bear". Consequently, it encountered a deep crisis that threatened the continuity of its civilization.

"Adversity strengthens a nation; profound worries give rise to sages." In order for the Chinese nation to stand on its own feet and assert itself in the world, numerous pioneers have cried out in their impassioned elegies, lamenting their "heartfelt desire to fight the enemy but lacking the strength to turn the tide". Countless martyrs have made heroic sacrifices, "shedding blood for the righteous course, with steadfast revolutionary spirit". And countless pioneers have exhausted their strength to call for revolutionary action, striving to "pull the raging waves back and support the collapsing edifice". Unwavering in their resolve and unchanging in their original intentions even in the face of death, the Party has led the people to relentlessly struggle and forge ahead, all in the pursuit of paving the right path for China and securing a brighter future for the Chinese nation.

The value of light is only perceived in darkness, and the true meaning of revival can only be understood through suffering. After enduring numerous hardships and setbacks, the Chinese people's long-cherished dream of national rejuvenation has finally emerged from the shadows and now radiates with the brilliance of the sun. Today, we can proudly say to our ancestors that this flourishing era is as you wished.

China, marching on the path of progress, is a veritable "dream factory",

C919 large aircraft

Jiaolong manned submarine

China's domestically built aircraft carrier Shandong

pulsing with vitality and energy. A critical indicator of a nation or a country in its ascendant phase is the courage to envisage audacious dreams and the unwavering conviction and perseverance to chase and realize them. The millennium dream of moderate prosperity, the centennial dream of strength and affluence, the dreams of space exploration and deep-sea exploration, the dream of winning Olympic gold medals, and the dream of developing domestic aircraft carriers: countless once-unimaginable dreams are turning into reality, serving as the steppingstones that have enabled the Chinese nation to ascend to greater heights. Today's China has the great dream of rejuvenation hovering in the skies of the country's history, spanning over 9.6 million square kilometers of land and resonating in the hearts of more than 1.4 billion people, unleashing a powerful force that propels China forward towards fulfilling the dream of a rejuvenated China.

China, marching on the path of development, is a "magical house" creating miracles in the world. Historically, rapid economic growth in a short period of time has often been accompanied by destabilizing factors such as major changes in social structures, adjustments in interest patterns, and substantial diversification in ideologies, all of which can have a profound impact on

---

> **A Record of History Today**
>
> ## Sanxingdui Ruins in Sichuan Province Inspired Trendy Products that Went "Viral"
>
>
>
> Recently, the unveiling of six newly discovered sacrificial pits at the Sanxingdui archaeological site in Sichuan Province has attracted numerous visitors. The Sanxingdui Museum has responded to this public interest by creating a range of products inspired by cultural relics, including eye masks, face masks, keychains, and even ice cream, all inspired by the cultural relics found at the site. These products integrate elements of Sichuan culture, such as face-changing, tea culture, Sichuan embroidery, and long cards, which are highly sought after, especially by young people. The picture shows visitors enjoying ice cream shaped like a small bronze mask.

social stability. The notions of "speed" and "stability" are often perceived as a paradoxical pair, particularly in the case of large and complex nations where achieving both is even more challenging. China, with its expansive economy, has managed to compress the industrialization process that took developed countries hundreds of years to complete into a mere few decades. Remarkably, it has also succeeded in containing development-induced conflicts within a manageable range, thus maintaining long-term social stability. Many Western scholars refer to China's two miracles as the "Goldbach's Conjecture" of economics and remain mystified by the seemingly inexplicable "magic of the East".

China, marching on the path of progress, is an "upgraded cabin" revitalizing the charm of civilization. The Chinese civilization has been flowing for thousands of years, from the mythical tales of antiquity to the elaborate rituals and music of the Xia, Shang, and Zhou Dynasties, from the "hundred schools of thought" during the Spring and Autumn and Warring States periods, which witnessed a flourishing of diverse philosophical schools, to Emperor Wu of Han's "dismissing other schools and solely promoting Confucianism", and from the prominence of Confucianism, Buddhism, and Taoism to the integration of the three teachings. Refined by the passage of time, it has become increasingly profound, forming the unique spiritual ethos of the Chinese people and a unique spectacle in the annals of world civilization. The CPC has always been a faithful inheritor and promoter of this remarkable cultural legacy, harnessing its inherent virtues in creative transformation and innovative development, and imbuing it with contemporary relevance. Through such endeavors, the CPC has provided a more substantial spiritual foundation for enriching the inner lives of modern-day Chinese people.

As we look back on the journey through trials and tribulations, we can truly appreciate the beauty of the present. We have gone through "the strong pass of the enemy like a wall or iron", traversed "the righteous path in the world full of vicissitudes", and are heading towards a future where we will "ride the wind and break the waves". The Chinese nation stands tall in the east of the world, showcasing its thriving growth. Socialism has not failed China, nor has China failed socialism.

3. Great Manifestation of the Power of Truth

Marx, the "greatest thinker of the millennium", brought the fire of truth to the world, revealing the universal laws governing the development of nature, human society, and human thought, and illuminating the path to human liberation. This is an awe-inspiring peak in the history of human thought that

Statue of Karl Marx

Karl Marx's former residence

arouses revolutionary enthusiasm for the "struggle for truth" worldwide, from the West to the East, attracting millions of Marxists to follow, comprehend, and put it into practice, thereby opening a new stage of human understanding and transformation of the world.

The "great encounter" may seem like a coincidence, but in fact, it is a historical necessity. In the 1840s, the Chinese nation, plagued by internal and external troubles, embarked on a difficult journey to find its way. At almost the same time, the seeds of Marxism, originating from a small town along the Moselle River in Germany, gradually matured, guiding proletarians worldwide to unite and carry out a revolution to overthrow all old forces. The aspiration of the Chinese nation for rejuvenation echoed with the thought seeking human liberation. The seeds of truth from the West, once sown, created a wildfire in the barren land of the East, unleashing a powerful force to swallow up the old and nurture new hopes. Over the past century, generations of Chinese Communists have converged under the magnificent sunrise of Marxism, holding high the torch of great thoughts, and creating a unique path to save, revive and strengthen their country. The bright light of truth has guided the surging journey of rejuvenation and enriched the grandeur of thought through epic endeavors.

Marxism's scientific and truthful nature has been thoroughly tested and proven. As Engels noted, "Just as Darwin discovered the law of development of organic nature, so Marx discovered the law of development of human history." Through its materialistic view of history and doctrine of surplus value, Marxism has overturned the idealistic view of history and provided a scientific foundation for socialism. It has illuminated the path towards a better society and a brighter future for humanity. The victories of the Communist Party of China and the rejuvenation of the Chinese nation are a testament to the scientific and truthful nature of Marxism, as Aristotle's influence can be seen in Alexander's triumphs.

Marxism's people-orientedness and practicality have been fully implemented. The reason why Marxism is a "true scripture" with an enduring power and

Chen Wangdao translating the "Communist Manifesto" (Chinese Painting)

Early Chinese version of the "Communist Manifesto"

penetrating influence is because it cares for the people and takes root in practice, illuminating the right path for human liberation. For over a century, the CPC has been a "Marxist in action", using the power of scientific truth as an theoretical weapon to strengthen its original aspiration and mission, seek happiness for the Chinese people and to solve the country's problems. Through these efforts, the scientific theory of Marxism has been deeply imprinted in the hearts of hundreds of millions of Chinese people and firmly rooted in the vast land of China.

Marxism's openness and relevance to the times have been fully manifested.

Marx did not provide any dogmatic prescriptions or specific portraits of the future society. He even believed that he was not fit to devise "the future menu of a small restaurant". Marxism has never been closed or rigid; rather, it is a theory that constantly evolves, enriched and developed in response to the changing needs of reality. Chinese Marxists have upheld the true essence of scientific theory while bravely innovating and adapting to the development of practice and the times. They have created a "Chinese version" of Marxism with national characteristics and contemporary relevance, enabling the living soul of Marxism to forever maintain its youthful vigor in the East.

Over the past century, Marxism has been intertwined with the fate of the Communist Party of China and the Chinese nation, unfolding a great story of a scientific theory with a century-old political party and an ancient nation. This stirring history reveals that at the fundamental level, the capability of the Party and the strengths of socialism with Chinese characteristics are attributable to the fact that Marxism works. The key to the effectiveness of Marxism is that the Communist Party of China and socialism with Chinese characteristics have infused Marxism with new vitality, demonstrating a stronger life force in providing answers to the world's questions and addressing the issues of the times.

4. Profound Impact on World Progress

China, as one of the world's "four major ancient civilizations" and "cradles of three major axial civilizations", was once at the forefront of human progress in astronomy, calendar, humanistic thought, political systems, material production, science and technology, literature, and art, making remarkable contributions to the advancement of civilization. As noted by the English philosopher Francis Bacon, China's great inventions such as gunpowder and the compass have unparallelly transformed the look of the world. However, since the Ming Dynasty, China has diverged from the world's developmental trends. Especially after the Opium War, a huge "intergenerational gap" emerged between China and advanced countries, and China was once seen as a "mistake and an impediment on modern civilization".

A Compendium of Knowledge

Three Major Axial Civilizations

In the context of human civilization, the Axial Age refers to the historical period between 800 and 200 BC, with a particular focus on the period between 600 and 300 BC. This time frame is recognized as a crucial period in the development of human civilization, marked by significant breakthroughs in various aspects of human existence. The regions where the Axial Age occurred are located around the latitude of approximately 30 degrees north. It is widely accepted that three major axial civilizations emerged in different regions of the world during this period, namely the Chinese pre-Qin civilization, the ancient Greek civilization, and the ancient Indian civilization.

The CPC emerged amidst the great tide of human liberation. Since its inception, the Party has closely linked the process of changing the fate of China with the global trend of promoting peace and development. The CPC has resolutely undertaken the noble mission of saving the Chinese nation from suffering and shouldered the sacred responsibility of advancing human civilization. In the arduous journey of "seeking happiness for the people and rejuvenation for the Chinese nation", the CPC has always adhered to the action value of "we are not alone on the Great Way and the whole world is one family" and promoted the "revolution" of world history through the "rotation" of centennial struggle. It has profoundly altered the trajectory and pattern of global development and made invaluable contributions to advancing human progress and pursuing a harmonious world.

The CPC has promoted world revolution through national democratic revolution. After modern China became integrated into the international system, the Chinese revolution was tied to the "chariot" of world revolution. From the onset to the conclusion of the New Democratic Revolution, it was closely intertwined with changes in the global struggle. In the 28 years of revolutionary struggle led by the CPC, whether it was proposing the anti-imperialist and anti-feudal democratic revolutionary program, crushing the warlord forces supported by foreign powers, fighting against Japanese invaders, or overthrowing the ruling of Chiang Kai-shek supported by US imperialists, they all constituted crucial components of the global national democratic revolution. The triumph of the Chinese revolution significantly fortified the international force of justice and propelled the historical process of world revolution.

The CPC has pioneered a new path for civilization through its own exploration. China's remarkable success in development has sparked discussions about "China wave", "China horizon" and "China era". Behind these awe-inspiring remarks lies not only the exponential growth of a country in terms of its economic size, but also the emergence of a unique path to modernization and a fusion effect brought about by a new form of civilization. The path of modernization, spearheaded by the CPC, takes human-centered modernization as its core value. It combines the compressibility of time and space, the sustainability of development, the comprehensiveness of structures, and the coordination of elements. This has brought about not only a change in outcomes but also an innovative model. While Western modernization is facing significant challenges, the Chinese-style modernization is leading and influencing the world.

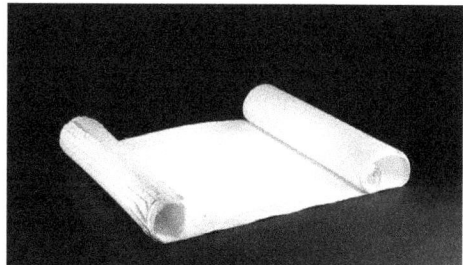

Compass, paper making, gunpowder, and movable type printing

The CPC had led the future of humanity with grand vision. In this great era of great changes and a global family, we need great wisdom, great aspirations, and a broad vision. As human history becomes increasingly intertwined with world history, nations and countries are becoming ever more interconnected, sharing common interests and facing common challenges. This has been profoundly demonstrated during the global pandemic. In this context, General Secretary Xi Jinping, with a global perspective and a commitment to the common interests of all people, transcends national, ethnic, cultural, and ideological boundaries. He has proposed the promotion of building a community with a shared future for mankind and the advancement of the common values of humanity. This forward-looking vision points out the way forward in addressing major global challenges and illuminates a promising future for human development and progress.

The Chinese nation has been characterized as a nation "with a righteous heart for mankind", and China as a country that "should make significant contributions to the welfare of humanity", while the Communist Party of China as "a political party that strives for the cause of human progress". Over the past century, the CPC has dedicated itself to the pursuit of a just and righteous cause, benefiting not only its own development but also the world. It has fulfilled its solemn promises with consistent practical actions. The CPC's work has been etched in the annals of human history, and it will continue to shape the future of humanity.

5. Forging of an Advanced Political Party Through Trials and Tribulations

In history, great events that open up new horizons often start inconspicuously, sometimes as trivial as the end of a thread in the fabric of time. A hundred years ago, on an ordinary day, in an ordinary alley in Shanghai and on a red boat on Nanhu Lake in Jiaxing, a group of Chinese Communists, with an average age of 28, convened in secret for the first congress and announced the birth of the CPC. The delegates attending the meeting were unknown "ordinary individuals" in society, but they harbored great aspirations. With

The site of the First National Congress of the CPC

The Red Boat at Nanhu Lake, Jiaxing, Zhejiang Province

their boldness and ambitious vision to change the fate of old China, they were determined to establish a new society on the vast land of China.

One hundred years ago, no one could have imagined that the CPC would become the world's largest ruling party with over 95 million members and significant global influence. Under the CPC's leadership, the fate of the Chinese nation has undergone a historic transformation, resulting in a radical change in the face of socialist China. The country's over 1.4 billion people are now able to enjoy a prosperous and contented life. What has brought about these changes in China? What has shaped the Communist Party of China? The answers can be found in the history of the Party's own construction.

Through countless trials and tribulations, the CPC has emerged stronger than ever. From 1921 to 2021, from Shikumen (stone-framed arched doorway) to Tian'anmen, and from a small red boat to a majestic ship, the Party's century-long struggle has been a crucible that separates the essence from the dross of history and a mighty river of time that sifts through the sands. Enduring immense difficulties, facing life-and-death tests, and bearing tremendous sacrifices, the CPC has been forged into a vanguard force at the forefront of the era.

Courageous and resolute, the CPC has been the vanguard of the times. "In vast China, who can be the steadfast pillar amidst the currents?" At a time when old China was lost and helpless, and a "storm concealing the homeland in darkness" seemed inescapable, the CPC stepped forward, bravely assuming the role of the pioneer in changing the fate of the Chinese people and leading the rejuvenation of the Chinese nation. The Party has led the people to rise up in the face of adversity, grow amidst challenges and move forward through reforms, achieving one victory after another. It has won a bright future for the Chinese nation, bringing peace and prosperity to China. The Communist Party of China, as the leader and vanguard of China, has inscribed its remarkable achievements on the Chinese land, deserving the honor of the country, the people, history, and the times.

The CPC has forged a resolute character and strengthened itself over time. From its early days with just a few dozen members, to seizing political power with over 4 million members, and now celebrating its centenary with more than 95 million members, the Party has grown from small to large and from weak to strong. Despite the changes and challenges of the times, the Party remains youthful and vibrant, continuously breaking new ground. The fundamental reason behind this lies in the distinctive political character the Party has forged through its long-term endeavors. It has shown the courage to engage in self-revolution and the ability to adeptly rectify mistakes and learn from them. It is through this process of reforming the old and nurturing the new that the Party achieves self-renewal and self-transcendence. As the saying goes, "He who conquers others is strong; he who conquers himself is mighty." It is precisely because the Party has repeatedly picked up the scalpel to remove its own maladies that it has been able to continually rejuvenate itself and possess the power to conquer any challenge.

The CPC has stood at the forefront of the times. The past century has been marked by unprecedented developments in our understanding of the world and our ability to transform it. The world has witnessed two devastating

---

A Record of History Today

The Long March National Cultural Park in Shihao Town

The CPC has always upheld the spirit of the times. "The heroic spirit fills the heavens and the earth, still resolute through the ages." Over the past century, Chinese Communists have relied on their indomitable spirit to strengthen their resolve. In this extraordinary journey, they have forged a spiritual lineage rooted in the great political party and narrates the century-long epic of the Chinese nation's great spirit. The CPC stands tall in the rich spiritual nourishment it has received, integrating its spirit into the nation's long history and merging it into the lofty righteousness that influences the world.

A Compendium of Knowledge

The Great Spirit of the Party's Founding and the Long Line of Inspiring Principles for Chinese Communists

On July 1, 2021, General Secretary Xi Jinping expounded the great founding spirit of the Party in a Speech at a Ceremony Marking the Centenary of the Communist Party of China. The great founding spirit of the Party is comprised of the following principles: upholding truth and ideals, staying true to our original aspiration and founding mission, fighting bravely without fear of sacrifice, and remaining loyal to the Party and faithful to the people. Throughout the past century, the Party has utilized the great founding spirit of the Party as a foundational element in developing a long line of inspiring principles for Chinese Communists, encompassing the spirit of the first revolutionary base in the Jinggang Mountains, the spirit of the Soviet Areas, the spirit of the Long March, the spirit of the Zunyi meeting, the spirit of Yan'an, the spirit of the resistance against Japanese aggression, the spirit of the revolutionaries at the Red Crag, the spirit of Xibaipo, the great spirit in the War to Resist US Aggression and Aid Korea, the spirit of "Two Bombs and One Satellite", the spirit of reform and opening up, the spirit of the Special Administrative Region, the spirit of combating the flood, the spirit of disaster relief, the spirit of poverty eradication, and the spirit of combating COVID-19, among others.

world wars, the evolution and iteration of two scientific and technological revolutions, the struggle and competition between two social systems, and the spread and ravages of two global pandemics, among other significant events. The scope, rapidity, and depth of these changes are unprecedented in human history. "The tide riders surf the currents." In such an unprecedented and dramatic era of change, the CPC has continuously enhanced its ability to navigate complex situations, perceive the changes of the times, follow the tide, and act in accordance with the general trend. It has been able to secure the historical initiative and strategic dominance of the Chinese revolution, construction, and reform, and has made great strides in advancing the process of national rejuvenation.

Standing atop a high mountain, one can see the rushing rivers; upon the peaks of towering mountains, one can feel the mighty winds. Similarly, at this special juncture in time, we can clearly perceive that the centenary of the CPC is a historical process in which an ancient nation has pursued its millennium-long dream and embarked on the path to national rejuvenation. It is a temporal and spatial journey for a great Eastern country to reclaim its former glory and assert itself at the center of the world stage. This magnificent epic, spanning across time and space, is unparalleled both in the history of the Chinese nation and in the history of the world. It shines brilliantly like the stars, resonates with the past and present, and stands alongside the heavens and earth, radiating alongside the sun and the moon.

Chapter XI

The Echoes of History Enlighten the Future

— The CPC's endeavors over the past century reveal why we were successful in the past and how we can continue to succeed in the future.

"History doesn't repeat itself, but it does rhyme." When looking back on a period of history, we should not dwell on specific events, but focus on valuable lessons from the depths of history that can inform the present and shape the future. This is the true significance of understanding history. The CPC, which has experienced the vicissitudes of a century, has gone through numerous trials and tribulations, setbacks and resurgences, presenting a series of thrilling and captivating historical dramas. Today, as we reflect on the great historical drama of the Party's century-long struggle, what resounds in our hearts is the historical blossoms nurtured by countless predecessors with their blood and sweat, and the light of wisdom that transcends time and space, illuminates the present, and looks far into the future.

Through storms and hardships, we forge ahead; the path is as solid as a grindstone, leading us straight forward. The past century has witnessed the glorious triumphs amidst trials and tribulations, and the resplendent honor earned through bloodshed. It is a testament to the unshakable pursuit and endeavors of the Party, the tribulations and awakening of the nation, and the rapid development and changes of the country. Over the past century, the sufferings endured, challenges faced, and miracles created by the Party, the nation, and the country are rarely seen in the world. However, all the gains and losses, successes and failures, rises and falls, and victories and defeats are precious spiritual wealth. They continuously enrich our wisdom and courage, empowering the Party to lead the Chinese people with unwavering confidence towards the future.

1. Valuable Experiences as Spiritual Wealth

Historical experiences, as the result of human practical activities, is highly beneficial for people to gain wisdom, understand patterns, and guide actions. Throughout history, both in China and around the world, wise leaders have always placed great emphasis on reviewing historical lessons to find the path to success. As the proverb goes, "Using copper as a mirror allows us to adjust the clothes; studying the experience of others helps us to understand gains and losses; reviewing the past enables us to learn about the law governing the evolution of history."

The Marxist political parties have a fine tradition of reviewing history, summarizing experiences, and deriving systematic understandings from it. The CPC has always attached great importance to and excelled in summarizing experience, finding the right direction for progress through the application of historical experience. In 1965, when Mao Zedong met with Li Zongren and his wife upon their return from overseas, he asked Cheng Siyuan, who was accompanying him, "Do you know how I make a living?" Cheng was momentarily at a loss for words. Mao then said meaningfully, "I make a living by summing up experiences. In the past, after each battle fought by the PLA, we always reviewed the experiences so that we could capitalize on our strengths, overcome our weaknesses, and then proceed lightly and swiftly to advance from one victory to the next."

The Sixteen-Character Formula

The sixteen-character formula refers to the guiding principles of guerrilla warfare employed by the Chinese Workers' and Peasants' Red Army during the Agrarian Revolutionary War. The main principles of the sixteen-character formula are as follows: "The enemy advances, we retreat; the enemy camps, we harass; the enemy tires, we attack; the enemy retreats, we pursue."

The Ten Major Principles of Operation

The Ten Major Principles of Operation were proposed by Mao Zedong in December 1947 and can be summarized as follows:

1. Attack dispersed, isolated enemy forces first; attack concentrated, strong enemy forces later.

2. Take small and medium cities and extensive rural areas first; take big cities later.

3. Make wiping out the enemy's effective strength our main objective; do not make holding or seizing a city or place our main objective.

4. In every battle, concentrate an absolutely superior force, encircle the enemy forces completely, strive to wipe them out thoroughly and do not let any escape from the net.

5. Fight no battle unprepared, fight no battle you are not sure of winning; make every effort to be well prepared for each battle, make every effort to ensure victory in the given set of conditions as between the enemy and ourselves.

6. Give full play to our style of fighting—courage in battle, no fear of sacrifice, no fear of fatigue, and continuous fighting.

7. Strive to wipe out the enemy through mobile warfare. At the same time, pay attention to the tactics of positional attack and capture enemy fortified points and cities.

8. With regard to attacking cities, resolutely seize all enemy fortified points and cities which are weakly defended. Seize at opportune moments all enemy fortified points and cities defended with moderate strength, provided circumstances permit. As for strongly defended enemy fortified points and cities, wait till conditions are ripe and then take them.

9. Replenish our strength with all the arms and most of the personnel captured from the enemy.

10. Make good use of the intervals between campaigns to rest, train and consolidate our troops.

A Compendium of Knowledge

Ten Major Relationships

The Ten Major Relationships, proposed by Mao Zedong in 1956, are a set of significant relationships that must be handled effectively during socialist construction. They include the relationships between heavy industry on the one hand and light industry and agriculture on the other; between industry in the coastal regions and industry in the interior; between economic construction and defense; between the state, the units of production and individual producers; between the central authorities and the local governments; between the Han and ethnic minority groups; between the Party and the non-Party; between revolution and counter-revolution; between right and wrong; and between China and other countries.

Looking back on the Party's centennial history, one can see the shining sparks of wisdom in the valuable experiences, which, with profound ideas and clear guidance, provide deep inspirations to people. The Party's incisive summaries of practical experience, which are the secret to the flourishing development of the Party and the country, are embodied in "The Sixteen-Character Formula" for guerrilla warfare of the Red Army at its inception, the "Ten Major Principles Of Operation" to win the battlefield, the appropriate handling of the "Ten Major Relationships" in China's socialist construction, the adherence to the "Four Cardinal Principles", the "Eight Commitments" to stay true to the founding mission proposed on the 95th anniversary of the founding of the CPC, and the "Nine Musts" we must adhere to to learn from history and to shape the future put forward at the centennial celebration of the founding of the CPC.

The Resolution adopted at the Sixth Plenary Session of the 19th CPC Central Committee builds upon the previous experience and achievement. It represents the essence of a century of historical experience and the wisdom accumulated through decades of struggle. The Resolution summarizes ten pieces of major historical experience: upholding the Party's leadership, putting the people first, advancing theoretical innovation, staying independent, following the Chinese path, maintaining a global vision, breaking new ground, standing up for ourselves, promoting the united front, and remaining committed to self-reform. The ten valuable historical experience, summarized from past experiences spanning a century, connect various historical periods of the Party's leadership and people's endeavors. They embody the most universal, fundamental, guiding, and long-term principles that serve as the quintessence of historical experience for the century.

The ten pieces of historical experience form a systematic, interconnected, and integrated whole. With the leadership of the Party as its base and pivot, it sequentially explicates the Party's value orientation, guiding ideology, major principles, path selection, broad-mindedness, driving force, spiritual character, and strategic principles, and concludes with self-revolution. The ten aspects are interlocking and mutually supportive that facilitate coordination in the Party's basic position, basic viewpoints, and basic methods, and constitute a scientific system of the CPC's worldview and methodology.

The hardships of struggle are etched in the passage of time, while the radiance of wisdom is reflected in history. The ten pieces of historical experience were not bestowed from heaven nor copied from books. Instead, they were accumulated through the Party's long and arduous journey through trials and tribulations, containing both successes and failures, sacrifices and struggles, truths and power, and glory and dreams. They are valuable summaries of past struggles, representing the inevitable product of practical exploration and the profound insights left by history, which must be unswervingly cherished, upheld, and developed with the times.

2. The Foundation of Victory and the Path to Success

As the wind blows from the East and the tide surges from China, the reasons for the success of the Party, the effectiveness of Marxism, and the strengths of socialism with Chinese characteristics have sparked discussions. People seek to unravel the secret behind the Party's flourishing centenary and the destiny-changing transformation of the Chinese nation, hoping to explore the practices that can be emulated. The ten pieces of historical experience of the Party over the past century, shining with dazzling "Chinese wisdom" and emitting a captivating "Eastern charm", represent the "golden key" to unlocking the door to success.

From a broad perspective that transcends time, space, and national boundaries, and standing at the intersection of the past, present, and future, we can clearly see the profound significance of the Chinese experience. With a century of progress as the vertical axis and the destiny of humankind as the horizontal axis, the invaluable experience accumulated by the CPC reveals the profound truths of why we succeeded in the past and how we can continue to succeed in the future. Moreover, it provides a Chinese example for countries still struggling and exploring in confusion.

The historical experience of the CPC over the past century is the solid anchor that leads to the success of the cause of the Party and the country. Since modern times, the two major historic missions of the Chinese people have been to achieve national independence and liberation, and then to make

China prosperous and strong and pursue a better life, or in other words, to "establish the country" and "develop the country". Various political forces have tried but failed to "establish their leadership over the country", and only the CPC was able to unite and lead the people to establish the People's Republic of China and build a new socialist China. While developing the country was no easier than establishing the country, the CPC not only successfully developed the country but also led the people to achieve remarkable accomplishments, making the country even more prosperous. Both the facts of history and the reality of today have proven that without the CPC, there would be no new China and no national rejuvenation. Looking ahead, maintaining unwavering commitment to the Party's overall leadership, and firmly upholding the core of the Party and the authority of the Central Committee are crucial to ensuring that all Party members and all Chinese people unite as one in pressing ahead.

The historical experience of the CPC over the past century points out the only effective means to maintaining its invincible strength. "The country is its people; the people are the country." Of the people, by the people, for the people – putting the people first is what has guided the CPC from victory to victory over the past century. During times of war, in the prolonged struggle against the KMT, the Party's ultimate victory was fundamentally owing to the unwavering support of the people, who served as "an impenetrable fortress". In analyzing the reasons for the KMT's defeat, someone astutely pointed out that "the KMT had wealth and personnel and had learned many good practices from the CPC, but they could neither understand nor establish a close relationship between the people and the military". During peacetime, the people are the greatest source of confidence for the Party in governing and rejuvenating the country. They are the most solid foundation and profound strength that drive the development of the cause of the Party and the country. In the future, we must adhere to a people-centered approach and work closely with them, recognizing their needs and meeting their demands. We must stick to the notion that development is for the people, depends on the people, and its fruits should be shared by the people, pursuing common prosperity for all with unswerving resolve. By doing so, the Party will be able to lead the people toward new and even greater victories in building socialism with Chinese

The people supporting the front line during the War of Liberation

characteristics.

The historical experience of the CPC over the past century reveals the "pathway to success" by taking historical initiative. The tide of history is unstoppable, but individuals are not merely passive participants in it. With a profound vision, scientific judgment, and resolute action, individuals can play an active role by adapting to the trends of the times and proactively shaping the destiny of the country and the nation. Whether it involves promoting theoretical innovation, advocating independence and exploring the Chinese path, embracing a global perspective, or daring to pioneer and innovate, and whether it is demonstrating courage in the face of adversity or establishing a united front, all embody the historical creativity of the Party. These achievements are a testament to the Party's efforts to enhance historical consciousness, grasp the laws of history, and seize the historical initiative, providing the fundamental guidance needed to achieve continuous success in the Party's endeavors.

The historical experience of the CPC over the past century provides a distinctive approach to leading the era. Many resilient creatures in nature, such as eagles and pythons, undergo arduous and cruel self-transformation tests at a certain stage of growth. Those who successfully complete the process will gain a new life, while those who fail will face death. Similarly, for social organizations to maintain vitality, self-revolution is essential to achieve self-breakthrough and transcendence. This is exemplified by the CPC, which is one of the few major political parties worldwide that has been in existence for over a century and remains vigorous and energetic. The Party's perpetual youthfulness and vitality can be attributed to its courage to undergo self-revolution, its willingness to undergo painful reforms, and its ability to constantly rejuvenate itself, thus ensuring the Party's robustness. It is precisely through this "unparalleled martial art" that the Party has remained dynamic and energetic through a century of vicissitudes, always standing at the forefront of the times.

3. To Cherish and Uphold Over the Long Term

History is a continuous river of time. To grasp history, humans need to establish various time periods, whether it be measuring in years, five years, or ten years, or spanning a hundred years, a thousand years, or even longer, assigning special significance to each time segment. Standing at the intersection of history, people reflect on the past and contemplate on the present, summarizing past gains and losses and drawing lessons from experience to better move towards the future.

The CPC has experienced a hundred years of history, traversing a century of glorious journey. Today, as we stand on this significant historical horizon, we review history and summarize experiences with a sense of solemnity. This is not to find solace in past glories or to rest on our laurels, but to summarize historical experiences, understand historical laws, grasp the historical direction, thereby accumulating the strength and courage to embark on a new journey, overcoming all challenges and obstacles.

During the National People's Congress and Chinese People's Political Consultative Conference in 2022, General Secretary Xi Jinping grasped the new orientation of the times, observed the general situation, planned the overall development, and clarified the future direction. He reviewed the journey of the Party and the people in the new era and put forward the significant judgment of "five paths we must take", highlighting the "five strategically favorable conditions" for China's development. This profoundly reveals the crucial reasons for the success of the Party and the country's cause, providing theoretical guidance for a deeper understanding of the Party's historical experience in the new situation.

The Party's historical experience provides the intellectual tools to observe, understand, and steer the trends of the times. The current world is undergoing major development, transformation, and adjustment. Certainties and uncertainties are intertwined, with traditional and non-traditional security issues overlapping and foreseeable and unforeseeable risks emerging one after another. This has led to an unprecedentedly complex environment, necessitating an enlightened perspective from history and the wisdom of experience to refine our insight into the present and the future. By correctly assessing the situation and scientifically anticipating the future, we can grasp the historical initiative and promote the development of our cause with a clearer sense of orientation and awareness of the times.

The Party's historical experience embodies the fundamental guideline for winning initiative, advantage, and the future. Karl Marx once emphasized that there is only one science, and that is history. In this sense, history is the

Q&A

Q: What are the "five paths we must take"?

A: On March 5th, 2022, General Secretary Xi Jinping proposed the "five paths we must take" while attending a deliberation from the delegation of the Inner Mongolia Autonomous Region at the fifth session of the 13th National People's Congress. The five paths are as follows:

1. Upholding the Party's overall leadership is the path we must take to uphold and develop socialism with Chinese characteristics;

2. Building socialism with Chinese characteristics is the path we must take to realize the rejuvenation of the Chinese nation;

3. Striving in unity is the path the Chinese people must take to create great historic achievements;

4. Implementing the new development philosophy is the path China must take to grow stronger in the new era;

5. Exercising full and rigorous self-governance is the path the Party must take to maintain its vigor and pass new tests on the road ahead.

Q: What are the "five strategically favorable conditions"?

A: On March 6th, 2022, General Secretary Xi Jinping expounded on China's "five strategically favorable conditions" for development at a joint meeting of members of the agricultural, social welfare, and social security sectors at the fifth session of the 13th Chinese People's Political Consultative Conference (CPPCC) National Committee. These five conditions are as follows:

1. The firm leadership of the Communist Party of China;

2. The significant advantages of socialism with Chinese characteristics;

3. The solid foundation accumulated through sustained and rapid development;

4. The long-term social stability;

5. The spirit of self-confidence and self-reliance.

study of reality and the future. Many current events can find their shadows in history, and many events from the past can serve as lessons for today. In 1939, Mao Zedong summarized the experience of revolutionary struggles and encapsulated the united front, armed struggle, and Party development as the "three magic weapons" for defeating the enemy. These "three magic weapons" played a pivotal role in the Party's victory during the New Democratic Revolution and still holds important value in the current era. The Party's historical experience has been tested and proven effective through practice. It should serve as a foundation for our thinking, decision-making, and actions. We should draw nourishment from historical experience and strengthen our determination, courage, and ability to promote the development of our cause.

The Party's historical experience serves as the basis for judging issues of direction, principles, and right and wrong. The ten pieces of historical experience, condensed in just 60 Chinese characters, encompass the nature, purpose, direction, guiding principles, founding mission, and political character of the Party. It embodies the essence of the Party's century-long endeavors. The fundamental reason why the CPC has its unique temperament and distinctive character lies in the essential principles embodied in the ten pieces of historical experience. Deviating from these major principles can lead to directional and principled mistakes. Therefore, at all times and under all circumstances, it is essential to consciously take the Party's historical experience as the standard for judging major political rights and wrongs, and align ourselves with the standard to ensure unwavering commitment and correct orientation.

The Party's historical experience provides important guidance for the political consciousness, ideological realm, and moral level of individuals. The history of the Party is the most vivid and convincing textbook, providing the most enriching and vital nourishment. The ten pieces of historical experience serve as a compass for strengthening Party self-discipline, a sharpening stone for firming ideals and convictions, and a navigator for improving ideological and political consciousness. When studying the history of the Party, it is crucial to deeply understand the spiritual connotation of the historical experience.

We should learn from history to gain insight and understanding, strengthen confidence and conviction, uphold virtues and moral values, as well as put knowledge into practice to transform both the subjective and objective worlds. By inheriting the "red gene", continuing the "red bloodline", and carrying forward the "red tradition", we can embark on the Long March of the new era.

The bells of the century ring, echoing a century of intellectual thought. What lingers in our minds and leaves a lasting impression is not the fierce battles and clamor on the ancient dusty roads, but the profound wisdom and philosophical thoughts in the sky of history that touch our hearts. As we revisit the history of the Party with reverence and gain a deeper understanding of its experiences with devotion, we can strongly feel a surge of incomparable passion within our hearts and infinite strength beneath our feet.

Chapter XII

To Assess Greatness, Look at the Present

— What is the CPC of the new era and what does it aim to achieve?

"I dream of recapturing the Central Plains and reunifying the ancient land, the same sentiments and desires expressed in the timeless poem Xia Quan." For over a century, the Chinese people have had a dream: to break free from a history of darkness and humiliation and achieve national rejuvenation. This is the ambition of a great party and the aspiration of a major country. In the past hundred years, no matter how much effort we have put in, how much suffering we have experienced, and how many achievements we have made, they have all been for the purpose of creating a better China and a brighter future for the Chinese people, ultimately leading the Chinese nation to its rejuvenation.

Bidding farewell to a century of trials and tribulations, we now embark on a new journey braving the waves. Today, united under the leadership of the CPC, the Chinese people are filled with enthusiasm, charting a new course to achieve the Second Centenary Goal. As long as we hold onto our dreams and remain steadfast in our pursuit, the resounding steps of the Chinese nation towards rejuvenation will never be impeded by hardships and obstacles. With our sights set on the shore of our dreams, guided by our ideals, propelled by our faith, and driven by our unwavering efforts, we will enter the new century with the winds of the new era at our backs, ready to embrace the next chapter of our glorious journey.

1. Embarking on a New Journey with Courage and Perseverance

"Know thyself" is a topic that has been continuously pursued by wise philosophers since ancient times. It accompanies the entire process of human beings seeking to understand themselves and the world around them, delving into philosophical inquiries about the essence, purpose, and meaning of life. Similarly, the questions "what is the Communist Party of China" and "what does it aim to achieve" revolve around the purpose, meaning, and value of the Party's establishment. These questions run through entire theoretical and practical processes of the Party's efforts and manifested in the historical endeavors of the Party for the nation, the country, and the people. This is the magnificent aspiration declared during the Party's establishment and the lofty value to be fulfilled through its actions.

Time is the ultimate test of a political party's unwavering commitment to its original aspirations and founding missions. Over the past century, the Chinese Communists have remained steadfastly dedicated to the rejuvenation of the nation and the well-being of the people. Countless predecessors, knowing that they would not witness the day of national rejuvenation, selflessly gave their all to the cause. They sacrificed their lives and devoted their youth without regret, broke through barriers and forged new paths without fear, and willingly served as steppingstones and ladders for the great cause. With such indomitable faith, perseverance, and relentless effort, the historic mission of rejuvenating the Chinese nation continues to progress, revealing an unprecedentedly bright future.

Today, we have achieved the First Centenary Goal of building a moderately prosperous society in China and have taken a significant stride towards national rejuvenation. Looking ahead, we have less than 30 years to achieve

the Second Centenary Goal, with two crucial milestones: by 2035, China will basically achieve socialist modernization, and by the middle of this century, China will become a great modern socialist power. By then, the Chinese nation will stand tall among world civilizations, exuding an even more majestic demeanor and more towering stature.

However, the road uphill is steep, and the final stretch towards the summit is the most arduous. We are now closer than ever before to achieving national rejuvenation, with greater confidence and capability, but it will not be an easy task that can be accomplished without effort. The path forward will undoubtedly be filled with challenges and hardships, bringing storms with thunder and lightning. Externally, hostile forces will continue to oppress and obstruct our efforts as the Chinese nation moves towards rejuvenation, using every possible means to block and contain us. Internally, problems that have emerged in developed countries over the past few centuries have erupted in China within a few decades, presenting complex and acute contradictions that are difficult to resolve. This is a hurdle that cannot be avoided on the path to achieving national rejuvenation. Today's China is weathering the storm before the rainbow, and by pushing forward and reaching new heights, we will be able to appreciate the extraordinary azure sky of the Chinese nation.

As the river flows through the Tongguan Pass, it surges even more forceful due to the obstruction of Mount Taihua. When the wind passes through the Three Gorges, it roars with fury because of the barrier of the Wushan Mountain. For centuries, the Chinese nation has endured countless hardships, yet no adversity has been able to defeat us. Instead, each hardship has propelled the sublimation of the great national spirit, willpower, and strength. The Chinese nation, with its resilience, possesses the resolve to confront all difficulties until the end, and the determination to restore past glories and achieve new heights. The nation's yearning overflows, and its energy has been accumulating for too long, ready to burst forth and create the pinnacle moment of national rejuvenation.

2. For the Well-Being of the People and for the Common Prosperity

The CPC attaches great importance to the pursuit of common prosperity, vigorously promoting it as a significant goal following the achievement of moderate prosperity in all aspects. This has garnered widespread support and recognition in society. However, some people have raised doubts, arguing that "common prosperity is a global predicament that even developed nations cannot solve, and it will be challenging for China to tackle it". Others claim that "we have pursued common prosperity in the past, but it ultimately sacrificed efficiency to maintain low-level fairness, resulting in common poverty". By scrutinizing the Party's nature, purpose, and historical developments, we will have a more lucid and thorough understanding of these misconceptions and a more comprehensive and in-depth understanding of the Party's commitment to achieving common prosperity.

"To save the people from misery and hardships, and to rescue them from dire straits." The CPC emerged from the people and prospered due to the support from the people. Whether it was to conduct revolution, carry out construction, promote reform, or rescue the nation, enhance its prosperity, and build its strength, the Party's objectives have always been centered on enabling all people to live a better life. The history of the CPC is the history of a relentless struggle to fulfill the people's aspirations for a better life. During times of war, the Party led the people to fight against the landlords, redistribute land, resist the Japanese aggression, repel invasion, eradicate Chiang Kai-shek's bandits, and pursue liberation, all with the ultimate goal of overthrowing the yoke of the "Three Mountains" of imperialism, feudalism and bureaucrat-capitalism, establishing a new country and society that embodies equality for all. In times of peace, the Party led people to rebuild their homeland and establish the foundation for a prosperous future, undertaking reforms, overcoming difficulties, adhering to principles, pursuing innovation, and striving forward, all for the aim of continuously strengthening the material foundation of socialist China and enhancing the quality of life for all its people.

As we look back at the hundred-year history of the CPC, we recognize that the great achievements of the Party were made possible by the people, and the magnificent edifice of the Republic was also erected brick by brick by the people. It is precisely because of the profound strength of the people that the Party has the boldness and confidence to "see who in the world can rival us"

A Page of History

The Southern-Jiangsu Model Explored Typical Experiences in the Development of Township and Village Enterprises

The Southern-Jiangsu Model, first proposed by sociologist Fei Xiaotong in the early 1980s, refers to the non-agricultural development achieved by farmers in the southern part of Jiangsu Province, specifically in cities such as Suzhou, Wuxi, Changzhou, and Nantong, through the development of township and village enterprises. The photo depicts the Wuxi No.2 Knitted Underwear Factory in 1986.

and "overturn the world with boundless enthusiasm". People often say that the red regime in Yan'an was nurtured by the people of northern Shaanxi with millet, the victory in the Huaihai Campaign was pushed forward by the people with small carts, the rural reform was initiated by the 18 villagers in Xiaogang Village who risked their lives to press their fingerprints, the township enterprises were explored by the masses in southern Jiangsu amidst the waves of reform, and the new digital, sharing, and online shopping economies in the new era were driven by hundreds of millions of internet users. Today, the great landscape of national development was crafted by the hands of the people, and it's crucial that the benefits of national development are also shared by all the people.

The pursuit of common prosperity has been a long-standing goal of human social development. For centuries, people have aspired to such a life countless time, but it has never been achieved under the conditions of a class society. In slave and feudal societies, due to the low level of productivity, it was neither subjectively possible nor objectively feasible to achieve common prosperity. In

The digital economy, sharing economy, and online shopping economy are booming

capitalist societies, although social wealth increases exponentially, the flow of wealth distribution is determined by capital, and the exploitation of workers remains unchanged. Only in a socialist society, where common prosperity is an essential requirement and inherent objective, can all efforts be directed towards achieving this goal.

Today, the reason why the Party emphasizes common prosperity is determined by both our value system and the practical needs of economic and social development. As China has achieved the goal of building a moderately prosperous society, promoting common prosperity through high-quality development has become essential to building a modern socialist country in all respects. On the one hand, we must both expand and improve the "cake" by further freeing and developing productive forces to create more social wealth. On the other hand, we must ensure equitable distribution of the "cake" by handling the relationship between growth and distribution through reasonable institutional arrangements, addressing the issues of unbalanced and inadequate development, and unleashing the creative vitality of the people. This will inject powerful driving force into the further advancement of China's development.

3. Stay Vigilant in Times of Peace, and Infinite Beauty Lies at the Perilous Peak

The sense of vigilance is a thought process that goes beyond the current circumstances, enabling one to anticipate and prevent possible crises. For thousands of years, this sense of vigilance has been deeply ingrained in the Chinese nation. Ancient sayings such as "being secure without forgetting the danger, being prosperous without forgetting the possibility of decline, governing without forgetting the chaos" from the *Book of Changes*, " life springs from sorrow and calamity; death comes from ease and pleasure" from Mencius, "I wish to be the first to worry about the nation's woes and the last to share in its prosperity" from Fan Zhongyan, and "through vigilance comes security, through negligence comes downfall" from Zhu Xi – all reflect the spiritual temperament deeply rooted in Chinese people, vividly interpreting the unyielding and enduring vitality of the Chinese nation.

The CPC emerged during a time of domestic and external turmoil and grew amidst difficulties and setbacks. As a result, it has developed a strong sense of crisis and risk awareness, consciously learning from historical vicissitudes and successes and failures to remain sober and vigilant. Throughout the Party's history, there have been inspirational dialogues such as the "Jiashen Dialogue", the "Kiln Dialogue", and the "Exam Dialogue", which admonish the Party to avoid repeating the mistakes made by Li Zicheng, whose rule was short-lived and chaotic rule, and to break free from historical cycles. Even today, as we reflect on the past, contemplate on the present, and plan for the future, these profound teachings remain vivid and thought-provoking.

The CPC has been in power nationwide for over 70 years, and the rejuvenation of the Chinese nation has entered a long-term cycle of upward development. However, the risks and challenges we face today are more complex, extensive, and impactful than any previous period. There are both immediate and potential risks, including general ones and major ones. Major risks encompass economic, political, ideological, social, and natural risks within the country, as well as economic, political, diplomatic, and military risks from abroad. These risks influence and interact and with each other, dramatically amplifying the multiplier effect of risks to an unprecedented level. Predicting and responding to these risks have become increasingly challenging.

As human civilization advances at an unprecedented pace, people's interactions have become increasingly frequent, economic ties closer, and information networks more interconnected. Social development has also become more organized, integrated, and systemic. Some scholars have proposed that modern society has entered a "risk society", where overall human capabilities have been enhanced, but the risks we face have also been magnified.

The ongoing global pandemic of COVID-19 is a prime example of this phenomenon. In today's era of highly advanced technology and medicine,

A Compendium of Knowledge

The Jiashen Dialogue

The Jiashen Dialogue refers to the written correspondence between Mao Zedong and Guo Moruo during the War Against Japanese Aggression. In March 1944, Guo Moruo published an article titled "The Three-Hundred-Year Commemoration of the Year of Jiashen1" in the Chongqing-based newspaper Xinhua Daily, which analyzed the lessons learned from the downfall of the Ming Dynasty and the Dashun regime. Mao Zedong, who was in Yan'an at the time, expressed his appreciation after reading the article and warned all Party members not to repeat the mistakes of arrogance during times of victory. In November of the same year, Mao Zedong wrote a letter to Guo Moruo, stating that they regarded his "Three-Hundred-Year Commemoration of the Year of Jiashen" as a document for rectification and asked to be informed of any errors or shortcomings he identified.

The Kiln Dialogue

The Kiln Dialogue refers to a famous conversation between Mao Zedong and democratic figure Huang Yanpei. In July 1945, Huang Yanpei visited Yan'an and expressed his hope that the CPC would find a new path and break free from the cyclical pattern of history. Mao Zedong responded by saying that they had already found a new path, which was democracy. He emphasized the importance of people's supervision over the government, as it prevents the government from becoming lax. Only when everyone takes responsibility can the country avoid decline and collapse.

The Exam Dialogue

The Exam Dialogue refers to a conversation between Mao Zedong and Zhou Enlai before they entered Beiping (now Beijing). On March 23, 1949, as the CPC Central Committee departed from Xibaipo to Beijing, Mao Zedong remarked, "Today is the day we enter the capital, like going to an exam." Zhou Enlai humorously replied, "We should all pass the exam and not have to come back." Mao Zedong said, "If we have to come back, it means we have failed. We must not become another Li Zicheng. We all hope to achieve good results in this exam."

---

1 In 1644, which was the year of Jia Shen in the Chinese lunar calendar, significant historical events unfolded. On March 18 of that year, Li Zicheng led an attack on Beijing, resulting in the fall of the Ming Dynasty and the tragic death of Emperor Chongzhen. During this tumultuous year, the Forbidden City in Beijing saw the succession of three emperors: Zhu Youjian, Li Zicheng, and Aisin Gioro Fu Lin. Additionally, Zhu Yougui served as a regent in Nanjing, and Zhang Xianzhong declared himself emperor in Chengdu. This period came to be known as the "Five Emperors" era. 1644 marked an extraordinary period of chaos and upheaval in history.

the spread of virus transmission, the scope if its spread, the duration of its impact, and the depth of its consequences have been unpredictable and unforeseeable. As the pandemic continues to disrupt lives and communities, everyone is wondering when it will end, but no one can provide an accurate response. This perhaps has led people to have a sobering comprehension of the increasingly shared challenges and interconnected fate of human society.

"Life is less than a hundred years, but we always worry about the next thousand." The CPC has already passed the centenary mark, but only by being constantly cautious and vigilant can we ensure the eternal stability of the nation and the flourishing prosperity of the country, ultimately achieving everlasting greatness. General Secretary Xi Jinping has emphasized the significance of the "Four Not-Easys", urging the entire Party to maintain a sense of alertness and crisis awareness at all times. Embarking on a new journey of national rejuvenation and ascending to the new heights, the

---

Q&A

Q: What are the "Four Not-Easys"?

A: On January 5, 2018, General Secretary Xi Jinping put forward the concept of the "Four Not-Easys" during the opening ceremony of the seminar for newly appointed members and alternate members of the Central Committee and leading officials at the provincial and ministerial levels to study and implement Xi Jinping Thought on Socialism with Chinese Characteristics for a New Era and the spirit of the 19th National Congress of the CPC. The "Four Not-Easys" include:

1. After achieving success it's not easy to keep the entrepreneurial drive and be mindful of possible problems.

2. After taking power, it's not easy to stay frugal and restrained.

3. During peacetime, it's not easy to discipline officials, and to prevent corruption and extravagant life.

4. In the critical moments of reform, it's not easy to follow the tide and the people's aspirations.

Party must embody the heroic spirit of forging ahead in the face of greater difficulties. We must effectively respond to the "four major tests" and "four dangers" with unwavering determination and efforts, leading the people to overcome every obstacle and conquer every peak to reach the most beautiful and dangerous scenery that lies ahead.

With the long reins in our hands, we need not fear storms and vicissitudes. Standing at the pinnacle of history, we gaze far into the distance, witnessing the magnificent journey of national rejuvenation, which encompasses vast territories and surmounts all obstacles. It ignites our passion and fills our hearts with excitement. Although the path to greatness is arduous and the challenges are daunting, it only fuels our determination and enthusiasm. Glory has been achieved, and the future is being created. History always favors those who struggle, run, and strive for victory. Let us take action and claim victory for the heroic new era of the Chinese Communists and the Chinese people.

Chapter XIII

Soaring to Great Heights with the Support of Strong Winds

— How can we learn from history, work hard, and forge ahead for a better future on our new journey?

As we contemplate on history, we reflect upon the past century of our journey. One hundred years ago, it was due to the CPC that the national rejuvenation of China gained profound significance and momentum, marking the beginning of a magnificent chapter of "writing our own history for the past hundred years". In the present day, once again, it is because of the CPC that the path of China's national rejuvenation is filled with vitality and progress, embodying the grand ambition of "reaching the skies over nine thousand miles". The century-old Party has weathered countless challenges but remains youthful and vibrant. Behind it are the aspirations of the predecessors, and ahead lies the entrusted hope of the nation. Stepping on the ground of the motherland, the Party marches unstoppably on the road to rejuvenation.

Our journey extends to the sea of stars, and our feet carry us beyond borders. In this historic moment, we find ourselves in a great era. With over 95 million Chinese Communists full of vigor and courage, and more than 1.4

billion Chinese people forging ahead with vitality, the Chinese land of over 9.6 million square kilometers is brimming with prosperity. We have amassed a mighty force that surges like ten thousand rivers converging into one. This powerful torrent of national revitalization breaks through barriers and obstacles with an unstoppable momentum, surging towards the shores of victory with irresistible momentum.

1. Coming from the Depths of History

History is like a long tunnel of time and space that stretches from the past, illuminates the present, and extends towards the future. It serves as an "encyclopedia" of knowledge, experience, and wisdom inherited from past generations, forming a unique cultural memory and spiritual foundation of a nation or a country. As Marx once observed, "The tradition of all dead generations weighs like a nightmare on the brains of the living." Thus, historical ties cannot be severed, and individuals always move forward on the basis of what they have inherited from their predecessors. This holds true both in the past and present, both domestically and internationally.

China's history has been continuous and uninterrupted, stretching all the way to the present day. With over 5,000 years of civilization, 100 years of the CPC, and 10 years of the new era, these significant historical periods have shaped a nation with a rich and vibrant tradition, refined a party that has weathered various challenges but remained youthful, and advanced a country that has made rapid progress while remaining steadfast on its path. They have outlined the "grand historical perspective" of contemporary Chinese people, fostering a strong sense of confidence and determination for the Party, the country, and the nation.

The profound historical confidence is rooted in the more than 5,000 years of Chinese civilization. The Chinese nation boasts the world's most profound historical memory, placing the utmost importance on recording history through writing. The nation has passed down a vast sea of historical and cultural classics whose richness and completeness are unparalleled by any other nation or country. Events that occurred more than 2,000 years ago could often be precisely dated to the very day or even the specific hour – a feat that perhaps only the Chinese nation could achieve. Such extensive and profound historical accumulation has nurtured the rich inner world of the people on this land, fostering a historical identity marked by a strong sense of pride and a profound sense of belonging. It has also cultivated the spiritual strength of contemporary Chinese people, driving them to continuously learn from history and forge ahead for a better future.

The profound historical confidence stems from the 100-year endeavors of the CPC. The long history of the Chinese nation has been marked by overall upward progress, but it has also been a journey of ups and downs, twists and turns. The past 100 years of the CPC bear witness to the great vicissitudes of the nation and the country. From falling into a deep abyss to gradually climbing back up and making great leaps forward, it represents a concentrated history of the Chinese nation's indomitable spirit despite numerous hardships endured over thousands of years. Through this remarkable history of struggle and rejuvenation, we can perceive the Party's sense of responsibility and dedication to the nation and the country, as well as the continuation and expansion of Chinese civilization and history. Such an extraordinary and magnificent history inspires the people's heartfelt trust and support for the Party and strengthens their unwavering confidence and identification with the Chinese nation.

The profound historical confidence arises from the great achievements of the past 10 years in the new era. Critical moments in history often come down to just a few steps. The past decade in the new era has seen remarkable achievements in national rejuvenation, development, and improved living standards. The millennium-long dream of achieving moderate prosperity has become a reality. Historic eradication of absolute poverty has been accomplished on the Chinese land. The anti-corruption campaign has achieved overwhelming victories and been comprehensively consolidated. Environmental pollution has been fundamentally curbed. To accomplish these great feats in such a short period of time not only carries decisive significance in the history of the Chinese nation and the CPC but also deserves special recognition in the broader history of human society. The Chinese people living in this era are fortunate to witness and participate in the creation of this exceptional history, which brings them immense pride and honor.

"With confidence in ourselves, we can sail across a thousand seas." The Chinese nation, with a history spanning thousands of years, and the CPC, which has traversed centuries, have emerged from the distant corridors of time, carrying profound historical confidence and a heightened awareness of their magnificent culture. They will undoubtedly showcase the splendor of China on the global stage of the 21st-century civilization.

2. Welcoming the Grand Event and Forging Ahead to the Future

In the historical process of the Chinese nation, certain years have extraordinary significance due to special major events. The year 2022 holds immense significance for the development of the Party and the country. The CPC will convene its 20th National Congress[1], an event of great political magnitude and historical importance for the whole Party and the entire nation. With great anticipation from over 1.4 billion Chinese people and high attention from the international community, the CPC will determine the policy agenda for the next five years and beyond. The 20th National Congress will reveal to the world what kind of China lies ahead.

Following the grand commemoration of the Party's centenary, we eagerly anticipate the 20th National Congress with great excitement, looking forward to this historical moment of continuity and progress. Welcoming this event requires us to draw strength and wisdom from reviewing history and summarizing experiences. We need to sustain our passion ignited during the celebration of the Party's centenary and continue our love for the Party, the country, and socialism. We should uphold the spirit of unity and striving, and foster a strong atmosphere of self-confidence, self-reliance and forging ahead.

---

1   The 20th National Congress of the Communist Party of China (CPC) was held in October 2022.

The volunteers are teaching Party history in both Mandarin and ethnic minority languages

The hundreds of millions of Chinese people have full confidence in upholding the Party's leadership and steering the journey of national rejuvenation. Facts are the most persuasive, and the voice of the people holds the most significance. It is a scientific conclusion drawn from history and practice that the CPC is the indisputable leader of the Chinese nation and its people. Over the past century, the CPC has emerged as the standout force among various political forces since modern times. It has led the country and its people out of the depths of destiny, achieving earth-shaking leaps from lagging behind to catching up and leading the times. In particular, the new era has witnessed historic transformations in the Party and the country. Through reflections on history and comparisons with the present, the people wholeheartedly support and identify with the leadership of the CPC and genuinely love and admire the core leadership of the Party and the leader of the people in this new era.

The hundreds of millions of Chinese people have faith in following the Chinese path towards national rejuvenation. The path determines the future.

As Mao Zedong famously stated, "A revolutionary party is the guide of the masses, and no revolutionary ever succeeds when the revolutionary party leads them astray." In its long history of exploration and struggle, the CPC has successfully pioneered and developed socialism with Chinese characteristics, charted a unique path towards modernization, and paved the way for the nation's rejuvenation. The upcoming 20th National Congress of the Party[1] will provide a new, clearer, and more specific strategic plan for China's path and modernization, which will undoubtedly provide clear guidance and inject strong momentum into the cause of national rejuvenation.

The hundreds of millions of Chinese people are full of confidence in promoting high-quality development and achieving a new leap in comprehensive national strength. Currently, the world is undergoing rapid changes with increasing international instability and uncertainty. China's reform and development have entered a critical stage, and domestic development is facing new situations and new problems that have not been seen in many years. Both internal and external pressures have mounted. However, the firm leadership of the Party, the institutional advantages of the socialist system, the strong material foundation, the stable social environment, the confident spiritual strength, and the vigorous innovation and creativity have all contributed to maintaining China's positive development momentum, providing strong impetus and momentum to propel the country to a higher stage of development. People have reason to believe that the 20th National Congress of the Party will make targeted arrangements and deployments to address the challenges we face and will lead the country's development to nurture new opportunities in times of crisis and open up new prospects in the midst of change.

3. Working Together for a Shared Future

In his 2022 New Year Address, General Secretary Xi Jinping reviewed the glorious journey of the Party's century-long struggle. Focusing on the grand goal of achieving national rejuvenation, he earnestly addressed the entire Party

---

1 The 20th National Congress of the Communist Party of China (CPC) was held in October 2022.

and the whole nation: let us work together for a shared future.

The prospect of a rejuvenated and progressing China is promising. "The golden age is not behind us, but ahead of us; not in the past, but in the future." In today's China, the curtain of the golden age has been opened, and the trumpet for a new journey and a new era of success has been sounded, whether it is for the nation, the country, or the ordinary workers and builders.

We are the Communists on the front lines, the last ones to leave, the first ones to start, the least self-centered, the ones who persevere until the end, the quickest to take action, and the ones who care the most for everyone.

We are the workers bustling on various fronts: the dedicated couriers traversing streets and alleys in all weather conditions; the sanitation workers diligently cleaning the roads and enhancing the city's appearance; the hardworking migrant workers sweating profusely under the scorching sun; the skilled and meticulous blue-collar workers striving for excellence; and the crucial screws that link together the fabric of a manufacturing power.

We are the new generation of farmers sowing seeds of hope in the fields. We are the diligent cultivators who ensure that Chinese people's rice bowls are primarily filled with Chinese grain. We are the watchers of wheat fields who can see the mountains and rivers and remember our nostalgic roots. We are dedicated to the prosperity of industries, the harmony of the ecology, the civility of rural life, the effectiveness of governance, and the prosperity of public wellbeing in the revitalization of rural areas. We are the ones who find contentment in our peaceful and fulfilling lives, where our bodies and souls find harmony.

We are the scientific researchers ascending the peak of science and technology. We are the Space "business trip trio" exploring the vast universe, the scientific and technological pacesetters conquering key and core technologies and overcoming critical bottlenecks, the basic researchers persisting in our work despite loneliness, temptation, and obstacles, and the pioneers leading the way towards becoming a strong nation in science and technology.

We are the PLA soldiers standing guard at the border, protecting the homes and people behind us. We are "the most adorable ones" who devote ourselves to the purest love for China, the ones who bear the heaviest burden to safeguard peace and tranquility for our country, the first to charge forward in times of crisis, and the most respected ones who put the needs of the many ahead of personal interests. We are also the most unwavering ones vowing to protect the country with our lives.

We are the young students who "devote our youth to the Party and never let down the people" while also being "the pillars of national rejuvenation and the pioneers of a strong country". We are the new generation who hold dear the teachings of the Party and aspire to contribute to national rejuvenation, fasten every button in our life with determination, strive to contribute to our country wherever we are needed most, and hold our ideals high and view them as inseparable from the destiny of our nation. We reject the notion of "lying flat" and the trend of "rat race". We are the new generation who do not waste our youth, who do not let down the times, and who are capable of shouldering heavy responsibilities.

We are also the white-coated medical workers who head for the frontline against the virus, the athletes who fearlessly gallop through snow and ice, the teachers who safeguard hope for the future, the firefighters who courageously go through flames, and the community volunteers who exhibit boundless love.

Millions upon millions of determined individuals, running towards their goals, each with their unique postures and expressions, share the same dedication and dreams. They emit a chorus of resounding calls, urging us to forge ahead in this era. They freeze-frame captivating moments that touch us deeply and weave together heartwarming stories of ordinary act of love. Like countless drops in the ocean, their collective efforts merge into a roaring torrent. Like shimmering droplets, their individual actions reflect the radiance of the sun. Each individual contribution may seem insignificant, but when multiplied by 1.4 billion, it becomes a mighty force that shapes the future of China in the new era.

The past has passed, and the future has arrived. We have been inscribed in history, and we are determined to pen a new chapter. We hold firm to our belief that the Communist Party of China and the Chinese people, who have achieved great victories and glory in the past 100 years, will surely win even greater victories and glory on the new journey of the new era.

www.ingramcontent.com/pod-product-compliance
Lightning Source LLC
Chambersburg PA
CBHW061224270326
41927CB00025B/3484